This work was done within the framework of the Cluster of Excellence Africa Multiple at the University of Bayreuth, funded by the German Research Foundation (DFG) within the framework of the Excellence Strategy of the German Federal and State Governments - EXC 2052/1 - 390713894.

Susan Arndt, Shirin Assa, Mario Faust-Scalisi, Xin Li Hrsg.
Narrating the FutureS.
Speculative Fiction.
A Polylogoue on Kanuri Wahiu´s Pumzi

1. Auflage 2024
ISBN 978-3-96042-076-7
© edition assemblage
info@edition-assemblage.de | www. edition-assemblage.de
Umschlag: Hedieh Ahmadi
Satz: Hannah C. Rosenblatt | edition assemblage
Druck: | Printed in 2024

Eigentumsvorbehalt:
Dieses Buch bleibt Eigentum des Verlages, bis es der gefangenen Person direkt ausgehändigt wurde. Zur-Habe-Nahme ist keine Aushändigung im Sinne dieses Vorbehalts. Bei Nichtaushändigung ist es unter Mitteilung des Grundes zurückzusenden.

Die Deutsche Bibliothek verzeichnet diese Publikation in der Deutschen Nationalbibliografie; detaillierte bibliografische Daten sind im Internet über http://dnb.ddb.de abrufbar.

Susan Arndt, Shirin Assa,
Mario Faust-Scalisi, Xin Li Hrsg.

Narrating the FutureS.
Speculative Fiction.

A Polylogue on Kanuri Wahiu's *Pumzi*

Series: Postcolonial Posthumanism,
ed. by Susan Arndt, Weeraya Donsomsakulkij & Xin Li

Inhalt

Susan Arndt & Weeraya Donsomsakukij
Introduction: What is Posthumanism? 8

Johannes Jakobi
How Wanuri Kahiu's *Pumzi* Describes a Heroic Story With an Emphasis on the Role of the Antagonist 11
   1. Introduction: 11
   2. Procedure 12
   3. The Hero's Journey 13
   4. Interim Conclusion 16
   5. The Protagonist and his/her Relationship to the Antagonist . 17
   6. Conclusion 18

Shirin Assa
***Pumzi*; The Labyrinth of FutureS. 20**
   1. The Labyrinth of FutureS 20
   2. The Door of Past to The Future; The Aperture of Fiction from Fact . 23
   3. Static but Sustainable: No-Future's State. 24
   4. After Dystopia: Mapping the Future within Present. 26
   5. Realizing the Preferable Future 29
   6. Incepting FutureS on Both Mind and Earth – A Concluding Remark . 31

Susan Arndt
TransSpecies Regeneration in Wanuri Kahiu's *Pumzi* 34
   1. The dead end of critical thinking – and beyond 34
   2. FutureS as a Critical Category of Analysis 36
   3. Who is afraid of dreams in Wanuri Kahiu's "Pumzi"? 37

Katrin Köppert
PUMZI – Eine filmische Gegenerinnerung der ökolonialen Gegenwart 45
   1. *PUMZI* 46
   2. Der Traum und/als das Undenkbare im Afrikanischen Futurismus . 47
   3. Traumarchäologie: Das de/koloniale Naturkundemuseum. . 48

Mingqing Yuan
Towards an Alternative Epistemology in *Pumzi* 52
1. Introduction 52
2. Towards an Alternative Epistemology 53
3. "Dance the Other" and Intra-action 55
4. Conclusion 57

Xin Li
Becoming the Tree – Ethico-Onto-Epistemological Configurations in Wanuri Kahiu's *Pumzi* 58
1. Ethico-onto-epistemology: Being in Relation. 58
2. The Outside is Dead: An Onto-epistemology of Dualism and Separation 60
3. *Agency and Resistance: Entanglement of Matter and Meaning* . 61
4. *Toward an Ethico-onto-epistemology of Becoming* 62

James Wachira
Becoming a Tree: Allegorizing Kenya's quests to save Mau Forest Complex in Wanuri Kahiu´s *Pumzi* (2009) 65
1. Introduction 65
2. Barad on Phenomena 66
3. "Pumzi" and Afrofuturism 66
4. Oral sources 67
5. Speculation 68
6. Wangari Maathai`s activism 68
Conclusion 69

Oliver Nyambi
Signs of (and) Climate crisis: the Aesthetics of Wanuri Kahiu's Ecological Pedagogics in *Pumzi* . 71
1. The crisis of signs 72
2. The African gaze 74
3. Signs, symbols and the aesthetics of *Pumzi*'s ecological pedagogics . . 75
4. Conclusion 83

Dikko Muhammad
Anti-dystopia, Afrofuturism and the Woman World: Re-thinking the Future in Wanuri Kahi'u's *Pumzi* **86**
    1. Introduction 86
    2. Science Fiction and Afrofuturism 86
    3. Anti-dystopia through Dystopia in the World of Women . . . 90
    4. The Composition and Power of the Council 92
    5. "Pumzi" and Afro-futurist projects 93
    Conclusion 96

Raimi Gbadamosi
Blacks 'n Sci Fi **98**
    1. Science in the Future in Fiction 99
    2. Exclusion in the Future 100
    3. Why have Black bodies? 101
    4. Need for perfection 103
    5. Enjoy the view 104
    6. There is always love 105
    7. Black face in hyperspace 106

Introduction: What is Posthumanism?

Susan Arndt & Weeraya Donsomsakukij
University of Bayreuth / Assumption University Bangkok

Past, Present and Future are not merely spacetime that happened, happens and will happen. They are equipped with cultural meanings and materiality, (re)moulding and (re)moulded by several agents. The material-discursive entanglement among several different agencies cannot avoid being involved in power constellations, and thus, the histories that they produce are composed of silencing and being silenced. The notion of silence is critically engaged in postcolonial studies as a category of analysis that perpetuates the oppression of those classified as the other and thus sustains the hegemony of those who are not.

Franz Fanon summaries this process by saying that "[yesterday] awakening to the world, I saw the sky turn upon itself utterly and wholly. I want to rise, but the disembowelled silence fell upon me, its wings paralyzed. Without responsibility, straddling, Nothingness and Infinity, I began to weep" (Fanon 2008: 108). Regardless of an ability to be powerful and have an agency of his own to "rise" above the ideology and colonial expectation in the society, he is confined by being "paralyzed" to continue living in the oppressive system. The paralyzing of his wings implies his physical and mental incapability. Therefore, he is neither nothing nor infinite, but is constrained in a space-in-between.

This problematic practice is not limited within the human encounter among themselves, white versus people of colour, men versus women, but its ideology and practice are also extended to the ways in which humans mistreat and disrespect other species entities, who share the current spacetime with us. Due to this, the postcolonial studies need to enrich their visions to include the decentralization of the supposed 'centers' in order to surface the fact that otherness categorised in the multispecies space, is similar to the otherness in the human realm that, as Fanon argues, is not a mere object of the self, but is a subject who can convey what it really is and capable of.

A way to do so is to engage postcolonialist visions with the insights of posthumanism that move humans away from the absolute central position of activities, and instead, repositions them within a larger web of interconnectedness. This paper intends to pursue this approach by reading Wanuri Kahiu's "Pumzi"

(2009) as a possibility of rethinking a new futuristic interrelationship that can promote environmental consciousness as a way to counter environmental degradation, sustained by human-techno dictatorship that, in Pumzi's case, consists of water scarcity and deforestation in an Eastern African territory.

Towards A Postcolonial Posthumanist Vision

Postcolonialism and posthumanism share similarities in terms of origin and methodology of looking at the world. First of all, both theoretical lenses have originated in the Western academia, and second of all, they have been (re)examining the oppression and silencing of otherness as a way to give back the power of the other. The difference between them is the factors of being others. Postcolonialism, on the one hand, gives rise to the human other by offering various critique of white Western domination of the colonial other and its diaspora. Consequently, it intends to deconstruct the colonial modes of thinking in order to reshape human mind, decolonizing it from the Eurocentric discourses that have been perpetuating since and even before colonization.

On the other hand, posthumanism sets its goal to decentralize human position, and in a way, decolonialize the whole Earth by removing and challenging the absolute anthropocentric model of thinking which considers humans as the master of the planet. As Robert Pepperrell argues, posthumanism aims for the end of a "man-centered" universe (Pepperell 1995: 171). Therefore, the main focus of posthumanism lies beyond the essential value of being human, or to be exact, on reinscription of humanism. This is why it is "post"humanism that rethinks and moves forward to valorisation of non-human entities and their interconnectedness to humans.

Meanwhile, this posthumanist aspect can be criticized as a strategy to direct our attention away from the oppression of people of colour. As Sylvia Wynter (2003) argues, posthumanism provides a ground for further denial of humanity to some people who have not been treated as humans. In order to overcome this tendency of dehumanization, she insists that people of colour, women, and those considered as minorities firstly need to be respected as humans. However, as convincing as it is, Wynter's argument can be enlarged from a mere critique on priority within the shared historical moments to an important engagement of those in relation and thus are affected by this problematic interconnectedness. Therefore, dehumanization does not suit to be the first central question of how to deal with the hierarchicalization of the world and the contestation of human hegemony. Rather, postcolonial critics and posthumanists should also engage the determination of personhood in their thinking, aiming to redefine what it is to be agents.

By expending the qualification of having personhood while questioning the definition of agents, human and its position, dehumanization will be automatically paused and can be eliminated if the position of human is no longer holding the self-proclaimed centre of the universe. This mode of thinking of postcolonialism and posthumanism generates a postcolonialposthumanist vision that is able to propose new trajectories in which posthumanist approaches and postcolonial critics can learn from each other's aspects and histories, and thus, their merging vision effectively provides a way to respond to ongoing legacies of contemporary environmental injustice as seen in "Pumzi". Therefore, this volume is dedicated to pose posthuman and postcolonial perspectives, in given entanglements, on this short movie with a vision full of longevity.

Works Cited

Fanon, Franz. *Black Skin, White Masks.* London: Pluto, 2008.
Kahiu, Wanuri (Director). *Pumzi* Kenya 2009.
Pepperell, Robert. *The Posthuman Condition.* Oxford: Intellect 1995.
Wynter, Sylvia. "Unsettling the Coloniality of Being/Power/Truth/Freedom: Towards the Human, after Man, Its Overrepresentation – An Argument." *The New Centennial Review* 3.3 (2003): 257-337.

How Wanuri Kahiu's *Pumzi* Describes a Heroic Story With an Emphasis on the Role of the Antagonist

Johannes Jakobi

1. Introduction:

Left without any drinking water Asha crouches on the sandy soil. Any hope of somebody coming to rescue her is nothing more than a last effort of her will to live. Around her are only the dessert, rocks and the blistering heat. The sun beats down mercilessly, slowly snuffing out Ashas life. While the camera slowly fades away, Ashas impasse becomes clear (Kahiu 2009: 19:00-20:15).

When thinking about the end of "Pumzi", you might not immediately think of a prototypical hero's journey. Not least because of our viewing habits – that are strongly influenced by the happy-endings we all know from numerous Hollywood movies – the death of the protagonist is unusual to us. That's why a movie such as "Pumzi" does not, in the first place, correspond to our imagination of a heroic story.

In my paper I want to amend this misbelief. I want to show that it is possible to describe the story of "Pumzi" as a story of a hero's journey even so Asha, the protagonist in "Pumzi", dies at the end of the movie. I want to prove that Asha is a hero even if she does not have much in common with the seemingly invulnerable Bonds and Lara Crofts of Hollywood. Contrary to the popular belief, I will demonstrate that a happy ending is no indispensable presupposition of a hero's journey. Many theoretical approaches have shown that other features are determining if a story can be described as a hero's journey or not. Important is the structure of the plot. Consequently, every hero's journey is a story that follows certain patterns or stages. Every protagonist of a movie that can be described as a hero's journey – it doesn't matter if it is "James Bond" or "Nemo" – follows that more or less basic type of story.

As the heading indicates, I want to emphasise the role of the antagonist in "Pumzi". Every hero's journey does need someone that represents the "dark side"; someone that acts as an opponent. The interesting thing is that in "Pumzi" there is no villain. At least there is no figure that acts malicious and functions as the stereotypical antagonist such as Lord Voldemort in "Harry Potter" or Cruella de Vil in "One Hundred and One Dalmatians". Since "Pumzi" depicts a dystopic world in which water is extremely scarce, the movie surely concerns the interdisciplinary point of views of ecocriticism. I want to show that aspects that have to do with ecocriticism are displayed in a way that the environment itself can be described as the antagonist.

2. Procedure

There are different approaches to the subject matter. The "pioneer" of the topic of the hero's journey is Joseph Campbell. First published in 1949, his book "The Hero with a Thousand Faces" (cf. Campbell 1949) "describes an underlying structure that most mythological stories seem to share, which he calls the monomyth, or hero's journey." (Schell 2014: 307) In this work, Campbell describes 17 stages of the hero's journey that can be roughly categorized into three bigger units, namely "Departure", "Initiation" and "Return" (Moore 2017: 273-274).

In 1992, the American screenwriter, author and educator Christoph Vogler carried on Campbell's work and published the book "The Writer's Journey". He adapted Campbell's theory to the work of screenwriters and displayed his synopsis of the hero's journey. According to Vogler, a prototypical hero's journey displays twelve steps (cf. Kellinger 2018: 100). Nevertheless, a hero's journey does not indispensably need to consist of all twelve steps, "you can tell a good heroic story with fewer or more or in a different order" (Schell 2014: 308).

I want to show that "Pumzi" indeed features most of the twelve steps Vogler described – and consequently is a movie depicting a hero's journey. In my opinion, it is unrewarding to give a coherent summary of the plot before starting the analytical work. Instead, I will give the summary of small parts of the movie while simultaneously matching them to the twelve parts of a typical hero's journey according to Vogler – if possible. If a part of the story of "Pumzi" does not fit to Vogler's theoretical work, I will give special attention to this part. If those parts would become rampant, the thesis of this paper – the story of Asha in "Pumzi" qualifies as a hero's journey – would not be maintained tenable.

This twelve-staged process will be elaborated in the third chapter of this paper called "The Hero's Journey". Afterwards, I will give my attention to the terms *protagonist and antagonist*. In the previous chapter I showed that Asha is the hero in "Pumzi". She is the protagonist of the story; she is the one at the centre of attention. Her actions are greatly influenced by a goal that she wants to achieve. As I mentioned in the introduction, there is no character blocking Ashas desires – which would make them an antagonist – at first appearance (cf. Jacobs; Lorenz 2013: 120-121). Nevertheless, I claim that there is an antagonist in "Pumzi". There are several authors such as Lajos Egri ("Dramatisches Schreiben") or David Howards ("How to Build a Great Screenplay") that did do research on this topic that will help me with my work.

3. The Hero's Journey

3.1. The Ordinary World

"Pumzi" begins with an overlay that gives the viewer an overview of the location and the time the movie takes place: The events depicted are located in East Africa, 35 years after World War III, the so called "Water War". A young female citizen of the "Maitu Community" called Asha is living a desolate depressing life in what appears to be one of the last human metropolitan areas of the world. The sterile and futuristic space-platform alike habitat of the people seems to be only designed for one reason: saving resources. The world as we know it does not exist anymore after World War III; instead the soil is arid and the excessive heat renders a life outside of the air-conditioned platform impossible. A free self-determined life had to give way to a police state that tries to secure life of the citizens: Dreaming is forbidden in order to have no one being disruptive; wasting of drinking water is meticulously regulated, going to the toilet is not considered a natural human need anymore – it is seen as a possibility of generating drinking water through a purification process (Kahiu 2009: 00:00-03:50). According to Vogler's first step of a typical hero's journey Asha is shown as "a regular person leading an ordinary life" (Kellinger 2018: 100).

3.2. Call to Adventure

Asha works in the "Virtual Natural History Museum". One day she receives a box with no sender written on it. Instead, there are coordinates written on it. The box contains a sample of soil. With the help of her computer and scanner she analyses the substance. To Asha's surprise the results show that the soil is characterized as "high water content" and is not radioactive. After smelling the soil, she falls into a trance-like daydream that is heavily pivoting on water. She then plants the so called "mother seed", a relic of bygone fruitful times, into the soil sample and it miraculously begins to grow. Via video chat Asha asks the council for the permission to leave the station and search for the soil, but her wish is declined. Nevertheless, she takes an ancient compass out of the collection of the museum and starts to investigate (Kahiu 2009: 03:51-09:30). The second step "The Call to Adventure" is made as Asha "is presented with a challenge that disrupts [her] ordinary life." (Kellinger 2018: 100)

3.3. Refusal of the Call

This very moment the security force enters the museum and goes on a rampage. Asha manages to put the "mother seed" quickly in her belt bag and hides the compass under her working-desk. She is dragged away. As a punishment, she has to generate electricity by exercising on a rowing machine. (Kahiu 2009: 09:31-10:52)

Step three of a hero's journey primarily is about "the hero mak[ing] excuses about why he can't go on the adventure." (Kellinger 2018: 100) In "Pumzi" the reverse is true. Asha is not backing away from the challenge; instead, her surroundings are actively withholding her. Vogler describes such cases as an exceptional case of the third step "Refusal of the Call". The police state, here personified as security force, act as the so called "Threshold Guardian, blocking the heroes before the adventure has even begun." (Vogler 2007: 111)

3.4. Meeting with the Mentor

Soon afterwards Asha meets her "Mentor", a "figure [giving] advice, training or aid" (Kellinger 2018: 100). A toilet attendant hands her the compass she hid under her desk from the security force (Kahiu 2009: 10:53-11:13). While giving Asha this physical gift, she "strengthens the hero's mind to face an ordeal with confidence" (Vogler 2007: 120). Asha's courage seemed to be broken, but being again in possession of the compass wings her hope of being able to find the coordinates of the soil.

3.5. Crossing the First Threshold

She waters the seed from her belt bag one last time, enters a cargo elevator and manages to find a way out of the complex without being detected (Kahiu 2009: 11:14-12:03). This is the time in the story when Asha is "Crossing the First Threshold" which means "leav[ing] the ordinary world and enter[ing] the adventure world" (Kellinger 2018: 100).

3.6. Tests, Allies, Enemies

As she is now on her own with nobody to help, Asha faces "a series of trials and challenges" (Vogler 2007: 136). She has to survive in the desert, an environment in which "things are [naturally] more dangerous, and the price of mistakes is higher" (Vogler 2007: 136). First of all, Asha has to get out of sight of her community. Therefore, she climbs a tremendous wall of rock. She finds a waste disposal site that is used by her community. Since Asha is wearing no shoes, she uses old scrap of cloth to bandage her feet and ties another piece around her head to be protected against the sun. In fact, she shows "how quickly she can adjust to the new rules of the Special World" (Vogler 2007: 139), which makes her – again – a hero according to Vogler. For hours, Asha follows her compass, but she has to pay tribute to the pitiless heat. Regardless of her thirst, she keeps focused on her goal to find the soil and plant the "mother seed" and therefore uses her drinking water to keep the seed alive (Kahiu 2009: 12:04-15:18).

At variance with Vogler's doctrine, Asha does not meet any allies, sidekicks, enemies or rivals. But at this stage the occurrence of those characters is no indispensable presupposition of a typical hero's journey. They may occur, but don't have to (cf. Vogler 2007: 137-138). To the contrary: considering the uninhabited setting of "Pumzi" at this time of the story it would be strange if there – for example – was a sudden helper in Asha's hour of need.

3.7. Approach to the Inmost Cave

Asha is close to death, her legs are shaking. She looks at her compass for one last time and drops the gadget to the ground. From this time on, she leaves her life to her fate and indomitable will. Indeed, she sees some kind of fata morgana, a big healthy tree. She had seen this tree in one of her dreams before. Using the last of her strength she runs towards the tree, thinking of it as the designation of her journey (Kahiu 2009: 15:19-16:28).

In most heroes' journeys this is the point in which the hero "makes final preparations for the central ordeal of the adventure." (Vogler 2007: 143) In "Pumzi" however, Sasha has to face a "dramatic complication", which, according to Christopher Vogler, can be a step of the hero's journey as well. By throwing away the compass and only relying on fate and her will, Asha has completed "a further test of [her] willingness to proceed." (Vogler 2007: 149) She even decides to use the last drops out of her drinking bottle to water her seed which she planted in the sand. She then lies on the ground and provides shade to the seed with her cloth (Kahiu 2009: 16:28-19:27).

3.8. The Ordeal

This is the part of a hero's journey in which the protagonist "must die or appear […] to die so that she can be born again.." (Vogler 2007: 15) Left without any drinking water Asha indeed has no chance of survival. She dies. Asha now has entered the so called apotheosis: "Tasting death [lets Asha] sit in God's chair for a while" (Vogler 2007: 171) which means that "human boundaries" are no more limiting a human being. Instead, you might be able to "soar above the normal limits." (Vogler 2007: 171)

3.9. The Reward
This is why in "Pumzi" something "magical" happens. Out of the seed a big tree grows in the middle of the desert (Kahiu 2009: 19:28-20:10). Asha has made some kind of transaction. She sacrificed her life and therefore gets something in exchange (cf. Vogler 2007: 178): the certainty that there is still hope for living nature in the otherwise ruined world after the "Water War".

3.10. The Road Back & the Resurrection
According to Vogler, in most heroes' journeys there are two more steps: After returning to the ordinary world, some problems are still not solved. Therefore, the hero has to use everything he has learned on his journey and fights once more (cf. Kellinger 2018: 100). This part of the story is a "second life-or-death moment, almost a replay […] of the Ordeal" (Vogler 2007: 17). Since Asha has already sacrificed her life to the greater good those two steps do not appear in "Pumzi".

3.11. Return with the Elixir
The camera slowly fades away and the title of the short movie is inserted. Suddenly the viewer is able to hear distant thunder, a sign that a thunderstorm is approaching (Kahiu 2009: 20:11-20:22). Having seen the dried-out world of "Pumzi" before, this weather phenomenon is without a doubt an extraordinary experience and chance for the community. Asha's "success has improved the lives of everyone" (Kellinger 2018: 100). Her fearless and selfless behaviour eventually benefited the whole ordinary world and brings this hero's journey to a close.

4. Interim Conclusion

It has been proven that the story of "Pumzi" follows ten out of twelve patterns of a typical hero's journey in Vogler's sense. It is fair to say that "Pumzi" consequently can be depicted as a hero's journey. The first thesis of this paper therefore is supported: Asha is not only the protagonist of the story; she is a hero as well. In the following, I will concentrate on a feature of every hero's journey: Every hero "needs" a villain to fight against, every protagonist has to face their antagonist.

5. The Protagonist and his/her Relationship to the Antagonist

In the first instance, it is necessary to give a more precise definition of the term protagonist, since protagonist and antagonist work as a conceptual pair. Put simply, the protagonist, also referred to as the main character, is the person or group of people who the story is about: here Asha (cf. Howard 2004: 70). For this reason, the story is usually revolving around the actions and experiences of the protagonist who therefore is attracting most of the audience's attention (cf. Howard; Mabley 1998: 70). The protagonist's willingness to accomplish a goal such as revenge, honor or power is usually the trigger for the events that the audience get presented (cf. Egri 2003: 139). The antagonist is the force that acts oppositional and therefore is a stumbling block to the fulfillment of the protagonist's goals. In summary it can be said that the suspense of a movie like "Pumzi" evolves because of the „changes from consonance to dissonance between protagonist and antagonist" (Huston 1992: 111).

5.1. „The Villain"
In many movies there are *prototypical* villains such as the Terminator or a villain from a "James Bond" movie, for instance Dr. No (cf. Howard 2004: 14). He or she usually impersonates character traits that can be considered as negative and/or masculine: brutality, ferocity, assumption, arrogance, pride, ambition or enviousness (cf. Röwekamp 2009: 110). The villain uses and needs those traits to prevent the protagonist's goal. Therefore, he is the character that has to bear up against the superiority and intelligence of the protagonist who, needless to say, does everything in his power to achieve his aim (cf. Egri 2003: 145). The relationship between the protagonist and this type of antagonist and the resulting friction lead to a "crisis" that has to be resolved in the end (cf. Egri 2003: 146). Because of the clearly presented resolution of this crisis (antagonist and protagonist "combat" against each other in a plainly visible way) this kind of conflict is called an external conflict (cf. Howard 1998: 50).

In "Pumzi" there is only one external conflict. When Asha is dragged out of the museum by the security guards, they indeed act brutal or ferocious. But since they do not act self-initiated or out of spite, they do not fit the definition of a villain in most aspects. In fact, they "only" follow commands of the community's leadership ranks and are nothing more than henchman.

The leadership ranks of Asha's community therefore indeed fulfill some more aspects of a "villain". They are the ones who send the security guards, they literally forbid Asha to have dreams, and they do not allow her to leave the community. They are the ones blocking Asha's desires. But ascribing brutality, ferocity, assumption, arrogance, pride, ambition or enviousness to them would not be quite correct. Their methods are more than equivocal, but eventually they only want to ensure the existence of the community: Since the environmental conditions are hostile to life, every citizen has to do his bit. Breaking ranks and not contributing to the water or energy supply could have disastrous consequences.

5.2. The World of the Play as the Antagonist

Apparently, the antagonist in a hero's journey does not necessarily have to be a person. By being a "passive opposition to the goal of the protagonist" (Howard 2004: 78) the world itself, its sociopolitical construction, the system of the government or the way of life can be the antagonistic force (cf. Howard 2004: 78).

In "Pumzi" the environmental conditions are very challenging for mankind. Every human has to submit to discipline in order to survive. As a matter of fact, there is little room for "revolutionists" such as Asha. The individual's protagonistic desire is confronted with the antagonistic power of nature and its restrictions: Asha is not allowed to leave the community because this is considered to be endangering for the community but still does it. As a matter of fact, she goes on the adventure alone and eventually loses her life because of the environmental circumstances. Nevertheless, seen from a theoretical approach, she still wins this fight against the antagonist because her motivation was not to survive; her goal was to find the fertile piece of land – which she accomplishes.

In „Pumzi" the role of the antagonist is closely related to the theoretical term of ecocriticism. In Greg Garrard's *The Oxford handbook of Ecocriticism* there is a passage which states that "confronting ecological problems requires making choices and decisions which ultimately concern the very life of [all] people." (Garrard 2014: 155) This is exactly what happens in "Pumzi": Daily life is completely subordinate to nature. The most important thing is to provide energy and drinking water – at all costs. People are not profiting from the conditions, there are no agricultural areas or recreation zones such as forests. Instead, people after World War III have to fight for their life on a daily basis which makes the nature around them an antagonistic danger.

6. Conclusion

"Pumzi" is a thought-provoking movie; a piece of art that is broaching topics like environmental and industrial pollution, the importance of drinking water and its connection to world peace or the danger of all-over monitoring. Even if the protagonist Asha does not have much in common with the "shower of confetti heroes" that many grew tired of, this paper has shown that she indeed is a hero in a transferred or theoretical sense. "Pumzi" describes an unusual hero's journey, an impression that is reinforced by the unconventional antagonist in the movie: Asha does not have to fight a "typical" villain, instead the unpredictable, hostile environment, that replaces the "familiar" villain, becomes the antagonistic force in the movie.

Works Cited

Campbell, Joseph. *The Hero with a Thousand Faces*. New York: Pantheon Books 1949.

Egri, Lajos. *Dramatisches Schreiben*. Berlin: Autorenhaus Verlag 2003.

Garrard, Greg. *The Oxford Handbook of Ecocriticism*. Oxford: Oxford University Press 2014.

Howard, David. *How to Build a Great Screenplay*. New York: St. Martin's Griffin 2004.

Howard, David; Mabley, Edward. *Drehbuchhandwerk: Technik und Grundlagen*. Köln: Emons Verlag 1998.

Huston, Holli. *The Actor's Instrument – Body, Theory, Stage*. Michigan: The University of Michigan Press 1992.

Jacobs, Olaf; Lorenz, Theresa. *Wissenschaft fürs Fernsehen: Dramaturgie, Gestaltung, Darstellungsformen*. Wiesbaden: Springer Fachmedien 2013.

Kahiu, Wanuri (Director). *Pumzi*. Kenya 2009.

Kellinger, Janna Jackson. *A Guide to Designing Curricular Games: How to "Game" the System*. Luxemburg. Springer Science+Business Media 2018.

Moore, Michael. *Basics of Game Design*. London: Taylor & Francis 2017.

Röwekamp, Anne. *Zwischen Passion und Raison*. Berlin: mensch und buch verlag 2009.

Schell, Jesse: *The Art of Game Design: A Book of Lenses. Second Edition*. London: Taylor & Francis 2014.

Vogler, Christopher. *The Writer's Journey: Mythic Structure for Writers. Third Edition*. San Francisco: Michael Wiese Productions 2007.

Pumzi; The Labyrinth of FutureS[1]

Shirin Assa

1. The Labyrinth of FutureS[2]

Future is a labyrinth and as such an enigma that allures the imagination into – science – fiction and beyond. So does, at least, "Pumzi", a 2009 sci-fi short movie by Kenyan film director Wanrui Kahiu. Her 20-minute movie is a noteworthy literary instance, which meticulously depicts the salient complications of the future in contested and nebulous nets of futureS. In

---

1 This article of the same title was published in 2017. Assa, Shirin. "Pumzi; The Labyrinth of FutureS." In: Journal of the African Literature Association. 11-1: 58-69.
2 Herein, I make use of "futureS" and "FutureS" set afore by Susan Arndt, so as to respectively accentuate the multiplicity of it and the analytical purchase of the term. In "Dream*hoping Memory into futureS" (2017a), Arndt aptly begins her argument by advocating for both "futureS" and "FutureS" instead of "future" for two reasons; 1) futureS represents the polyphony of futures (in the wide realm of those that happened and those that did not); whereas 2) FutureS marks the "category of analysis", designed to analyze the performances of competing and complementary futureS. Also, cf. Arndt, Susan. "Dream*hoping Memory into futureS, or: How to Read Resistant Narratives about Maafa by Employing FutureS as a Critical Category of Analysis", here in this journal. Arndt argues against Barbara Adam's premise of the singular and thus, univocal use of future in "Future Matters" that is rather tantamount to using it as "category of practice", cf. Adam, Barbara. "Future Matters: Challenge for Social Theory and Social Inquiry" *Cultura e comunicazione* 1: (2010): 47 -55; cf. Adam, Barbara; Groves, Chris. *Future Matters: Action, Knowledge, Ethics*. Leiden: Brill 2007. In doing so, Arndt thinks in line with Rogers Brubaker's (and Frederick Cooper's) account on differentiating between "categories of analysis" and "categories of practice." On demarcating the categories of practice from the categories of analysis for social political terms, Brubaker opines that despite of their "close reciprocal connection" and "mutual influence" (Brubaker; Cooper 2000: 4), "unintentionally reproducing or reinforcing such reification by uncritically adopting categories of practice as categories of analysis" (ibid. 5) should be avoided; cf. Brubaker, Rogers; Cooper, Frederick. "Beyond 'Identity'" *Theory and Society* 29.1 (2000): 4-6. And also, cf. Brubaker, Rogers. "Categories of Analysis and Categories of Practice. A Note on the Study of Muslims in European Countries of Immigration." *Ethnic and Racial Studies* 36.1 (2012): 1-8.

doing so, the movie "Pumzi" unfolds a prospective story about the Earth and in*animate entities thereof with a posthumanist and holistic approach. By its apt consolidation of a Black female protagonist, "Pumzi" is a statement for the future per se, insofar as science fiction predominantly happens to feature white and mainly male characters as agents of future-making, a rooted tradition that more often than not blemishes imagination and is also bequeathed to visions of the future. Pumzi's protagonist, Asha, is the reminiscent of the planet's first woman and the oldest human skeleton ever excavated, Lucy, whose remnants were found in the vicinity of Kenya. Offering rebirth to a dried up and atomically spoiled planet, Asha translates Lucy's agency, or her legacy of survival, if you will, into a distant future from now and 35 years after the water war, known as WW III. More than being a researcher and a historian in the Virtual Natural History Museum of Maitu, Asha is a dreamer and a wanderer who connects knowledge, realities, setbacks, memories, dreams and hopes of both past and present. Owing to this Asha can detect a possible future that dissociates her from the told/available/designed future, scrutinize this alternate future's probability and take great pain in order to realize it as a preferable future in sincere conviction that this dream of hers will offer futureS of becoming anew; human as part and parcel of all un*animated life from soil to plant and, beyond technology. Her journey to an – alternative – future is nonetheless impeded by both those in power, seemingly technology, and the technologically controlled mass of humans, or rather humans' bodies. Asha's vision of future in one level contests the monopoly of future, in other words the lack of futureS, since Maitu's people are deprived of having visions for futureS; and at another level, it challenges the univocality of the future as envisioned by Maitu's state. This characteristic of "Pumzi" makes it a rich (con)text to talk about futureS as opposed to a singular form of it, which eventually requires one to unbundle the tangle of implication and connotation over the term future as a category of analysis: FutureS.

Future signifying a space-time yet to come (re)shapes the cultural specificities and, thus, is mutated into more than a sheer temporal indication and, inevitably, engages semantics, practices, objects, and objectives; equally impacting and forming meaning and matter. For instance, the technological devices are the embodiment of – the past's – "future" nowadays, molding new languages, meanings, cultures, etc. In effect, futureS are as much a linguistic concept as they are technological praxis, or political agenda. Residing in a conjectural domain, or in Wendell Bell's wording as a "conjectural knowledge", (Bell 1996b) engaging almost all disciplines from political science, engineering, medicine, biology and psychology to social sciences, diaspora, IT and technology, natural sciences, art, literature and so on, futureS, with the broadest of strokes, amalgamate the notions of prediction, anticipation, imagination, planning, hope, desire, and consequential actions in the ground of past and present. Concurrently, in addressing futureS, one cannot turn a blind sight to certain pitfalls that FutureS, in its morphing into an analytical category, grapples with; such as to romanticize "the future", regard it as teleology, and/or mistake it for practices of divination. In this context and suggested by Wendell Bell in "What Do We Mean by Future Studies?" (2000), with the pervasive need for futureS to be analyzed systematically and to be recognized as a category of analysis, a relatively new field of studies named "future studies", "the futures field", or "future research" has been ushered in 1996.

It was not before "1970 [that] concern with the future be[comes] fashionable" (Bell 1996b: 3) and even though "the Black Power protest of 1960s," together with "science fiction […]; the counter-culture, [as well as] the environmental movement of the 1970s" (8), to enumerate but a few, were among major forces which shaped the field, Black perspectives again both in terms of Black scholars and Black intellectual contributions were not integrated in the field. Hence, future – which was perceived to be a singular concept – too, unsurprisingly had been occupied by white heroes and has been mostly articulated through white gaze.

In line with the general agenda of other contributions of the Special Issue, this essay is aimed at discussing Black visions of the future, or rather futureS. In doing so, and in a dialogue with "Pumzi", these questions arise: How is the plurality of the future discerned and depicted in "Pumzi"? To what ratio do futureS interact and negotiate with one another? And lastly, what is Black about futureS in "Pumzi"? In parallel fashion, I mobilize the theoretical outlines of Bell to literary studies in order to better diagnose the ground upon which futureS in "Pumzi" are imagined – including the wide scope of possibility, probability, and/or preferability. Starting off with classifying different layers of futureS, the different types thereof and their entanglements are then discussed respectively. The concluding part in addition to a summary sets afore and discusses some of the political orientations of (and for) Black futurists, namely Wanrui Kahiu and Noah Sow.

2. The Door of Past to The Future; The Aperture of Fiction from Fact

The history of conflict over water dates back to the first civilizations, not to mention the key role that water has been playing for power distribution and political purposes, as has been documented by the "Water Conflict Chronology" by Peter H. Gleick, published by the Pacific Institute (2017). Furthermore, inquiring into the amount of remaining water resources on the Earth, the current trend of water consumption, along with increasing political tensions among power blocks – both in and between the nations –, it can be deduced how the mere possibility of a water war levels up to a high probability. The first shot in "Pumzi", through prolepsis and with a shift in time, conventionally introduces the viewer into the spatio-temporal of the narrative: Earth, East African territory, 35 years after WW III, "The Water War" (Kahiu 2009: 00:14). The narrative already accommodates two implicit layers of the future in this shot: 1) WW III, The Water War; 2) 35 years after it, which is, in effect, the present at Maitu Community; while incepting another level of the future in its concluding scene. The significance of the first shot lays in the fact that it bridges the factual world to a fictional one.

In his article "Choosing Your Future" (2003) Bell denotes that "[…] present possibilities for the future are real. They exist, even if they are only potential" (152). In fact, it does not take too much imagination to spot the potentials if one has a decent evaluation of the present condition. "Pumzi" is imagined based on the premise that the human factor is the main culprit in environmental depletion of natural resources in general and water supplies in particular, with irreversible effects on this planet's ecosystem. Moreover, the dire effects of climate change along with radiological weapons of mass destruction are not negligible. Such a gloomy picture of the future heralds the imminent devastation of planet Earth. Nevertheless, this by no means is to claim that detecting them is easy since the lines between the possible and the impossible are constantly contested and redefined, mostly in this era. There would be no water shortage or water war if the environmental balance of the Earth, its resources and the living entity on it would have remained intact. In this example, one can see the ways in which an impossibility *can become* a possibility, and how in (this) *becoming*, futureS are being born. Buttressed by the potential and the likelihood of a war of global magnitude triggered by water shortage, the plausibility of the setting in "Pumzi" is accreted.

The camera then zooms through a long shot into an isolated planetarium-like base, which is surrounded by deserts, and deserts only (Kahiu 2009:

00:16-00:22). Ensuing, it exhibits a series of documents before our eyes, which are taken from our real world right now (Kahiu 2009: 00:24-00:43). This fictional world, with myriads of factual references, reflects a future of a past with perceptible affinities with today's world. Although Bell suggests that one of the reasons that hinders an accurate understanding of the present condition and eventuates in confusion is "the rapidity of change," losing the track of "what is happening in the present, and what has happened in the immediate past" (Bell 1996b: 11). Yet, this does not seem to be the – only – case for "Pumzi" as it is implied that these environmental changes, which led to this abject failure, were disseminated and, therefore, could have been prevented. Headlines of newspapers on the effects of the greenhouse and scarcity of water remind of a past in which humans did not fail to foresee the possible and probable future rather to morally evaluate the extent of undesirability thereof and to take actions so as to prevent it: the death of trees and living under the sky. Simply put, although the data initially aimed at signifying a future of devastation, it later on served merely as a document to register human failures in taking initiatives to evade this future. In fact, the real problem veers toward the lack of responsibility in terms of taking responsibility for futureS, being backed up by power constellations that allow certain societies to continue living scrupulously – at the cost of others and their futureS.

Emphasizing the prominence of future thinking; designating possibilities, deducing probabilities, and evaluating preferabilities, and as a final step, acting upon it, Bell likewise elaborates on two possible stances towards the future: "[P]eople can deprive themselves in the present so as to profit from future payoffs that may never come. But the opposite is also possible: people can borrow from the future to the extent that they mortgage it beyond its limits." (Bell 1996b: 12) "Pumzi" narrates this latter position to the most part, while Asha strives to advocate for an alternative stance, which ultimately takes over; a dream driven life and an agency-oriented future. Having discussed the elements for future thinking, in the following, I intent to thoroughly delve into Pumzi's fictional world so as to investigate the correlation and the entanglements of futureS, which are laid out in the narrative.

3. Static but Sustainable: No-Future's State

After the brief spatio-temporal introduction of Maitu community, the camera rests on Asha; who seems to be dreaming. The virtual screen before her scans the dreams she is having: delightful images of a tree (Kahiu 2009: 00:49-01:14). Instantly, an alert shows up on the screen, instructing Asha to "take [her] dream suppressants" (Kahiu 2009: 01:17). She reaches out for the pills, takes them, and consequently, the dream is ceased – yet not forgotten by Asha. In her essay titled "Dream*hoping into the futureS" (Arndt 2017a), Susan Arndt elaborates on the entanglements of dream, agency, and hope as well as their significance for future making. She reads dreams as windows towards imagining futureS, and contends that what is being suppressed are not merely dreams, or future but futureS. Asha who sought refuge into her dream wakes up into the reality and walks the viewer into Maitu community. In "Pumzi", dreams – of alternate futureS – trigger agency for – Asha's – resistance against a now that suppresses dreams about futureS. At Maitu community, the apparatus of dream/future suppression is being pursued and controlled by technology.

Maitu's community, in my reading, is the concurrence of a "garrison state" and a "techno-dictatorship". In the first phase, to elaborate on the notion of "the garrison state", I argue in line with Harold D. Lasswell (1941) that Maitu features a possible and a probable "developmental construct" (455) for the future in the erasure of democracy and human dignity by the power block who "will have a professional interest in multiplying gadgets specialized to acts of violence" (465). As depicted in the film, people at Maitu are subjected to different forms of violation: bodily, mentally, and spatially. The garrison state, Lasswell (1941) also contends, "[…] will be distinguished by the psychological abolition of unemployment – 'psychological' because this is chiefly a matter of redefining symbols" (459). This is to say that "compulsion" (Lasswell 1941: 459) to serve the interest of state, or in other words to work, leaves people at the bifurcation of death or duty for which "[…] any tendencies, conscious or unconscious to defy authority" (460) is to be checked and controlled. In the beginning, Asha is compelled to report and to hold in control her impulses and as the time passes, this transmutes to confession and interrogation; however, due to the power of her dreams the compulsion is broken and a gap grows between the suppressor's interest and hers.

In the second phase, the apparatus of garrison state is translated technologically in a techno-dictatorship of Maitu's community. A techno-dictatorship, in Arndt's wording in her essay "Human*Tree" (2017b), is a state in which humans, without exception and regardless of their former sociocultural stratifications such as "race", gender, ability, and age are enslaved and subordinated by technology. The hierarchy pyramid is likely to be distributed upon the access to technology as a means of control and inserting violence. Before, human-dictatorship has controlled technology like weaponry and erased all nature in the process. Now, in "Pumzi" human is subordinated to technology in sincere eagerness to keep nature dead. In this dystopic setting the human characters perform very machine-like. They are dressed in identical uniforms and serve as kind of energy-generating machines (Kahiu 2009: 01:42 – 02:18). A voice-over, which is a hypnotic computer voice, addresses the Maitu's inhabitance, or rather, soldiers, collectively, and reminds them of their daily "share" for the community. Maitu's slogan: "100% self-power generation" (Kahiu 2009: 01:59) is the reminiscent of the totalitarian propagandas of fascism, communism, and National Socialism. Here, social interactions are kept at their minimum, and in turn, the dependency on technology is intensified; humans do not talk or converse, they barely have eye contact, their bodies are kept separate and attached to technological devices and mechanical machines. The orders are dictated in the electronic mode, and the suppression is a pill for daily usage. Technology overrules life and there is no trace of freedom, satisfaction, personal and social well-being, and barely a sign of happiness and compassion neither of hope, nor desire, nor futureS. The workout that Maitu's people are forced to do is deadly repetitive and static. The body movements are stagnant which indicates the ways in which the state of no-future is being incessantly imprinted on their body and mind; creating an illusion of movement and progress yet, virtually sustaining the condition of now.

4. After Dystopia: Mapping the Future within Present

Yet "Pumzi" through Asha's character advocates for a counter-argument: Although the access to future visions can be interrupted, futureS cannot be obliterated even at Maitu's regime circumstances. It is again the matter of breaking out of a mesmerizing routine or compulsions and exploring the potentials, which are the gateways toward change and futureS. Asha has received a box. There is no delivery note and hence, no answer to the question of who did send this seed of hope to her; as if it just appeared in the manner that her dreams always do. When being asked by her superior, Denti, to "report" the reception of the box with no identifiable sender "to the security and move on" (Kahiu 2009: 04:34), she insubordinates. Owing to her resistance when she was instructed to kill her dreams, Asha cultivates agency in her personality like the seed watered in soil which is the epitome of resistance; despite being cloistered and mut(at)ed for a while, they are true to their nature and, hence, grow as futureS. Remembering when forgetting is the remedy and resistance where subordination prevails. Thus, in Bell's wording, Asha "make[s] a virtue out of uncertainty in order to […] achieve a future [as a source of empowerment] that is better than the past and present" (Bell

1996a: 43). Instead of "moving on" which indicates ironically to confirm to the stagnant state, Asha lingers upon uncertainty and embraces the anxiety, insecurity and bewilderment that are concomitant to it and moves on. When seeing the soil sample, she examines its origin and soon finds out that it has "abnormally high water content" and "no radioactivity" (Kahiu 2009: 05:06 – 05:21). Thus, as is metonymically suggested here, the soil belongs to where another future kindles and an allegedly better life can emerge. A revolutionary possibility has just unraveled before her and a probability is budding, thus she cannot help but touch it. This is the first tactile interaction between two living entities as a result of which Asha faints, feeling her dreams turning to hope, and in a further step, a "reality". She dreams of being dropped into water, where she sees the roots of a tree and then, a tree in the desert. In fact, this is the same tree that she was dreaming of earlier, and ultimately being a metaphor for a promise for futureS. She awakens and begins her journey as the heroine of these futureS. Under the water, as one may assume, Asha screams for help, and the image of a tree appears as if to rescue her (Kahiu 2009: 05:46 – 06:06). This can be read as the renaissance of the heroine: death, baptism and, resurrection. Empowered by her dream, Asha reaches out for Maitu's mother seed and plants it in the soil. "I am testing its growth potential", (Kahiu 2009: 06:56) she informs Denti. Semiotically, in this condensed scene, the vigorous oscillation of Asha between possibilities and desirability of her future's vision, the past, present and future, human and nature, and the fact and fiction is anticipated and staged.

On briefing Denti (Kahiu 2009: 06:46 – 07:13) about detecting this possibility, and that it "could mean there is life on the outside", she requests an "exit visa" from the council, to which Denti aggressively comments: "it is impossible", and in more suggestive tone adds that Asha needs to "get rid of it" (Kahiu 2009: 07:07– 07:11). Whether she needs to get rid of the soil or her hope for alternative futureS is ambiguous, yet Maitu's seed is visibly thriving and her hope does not seem to be abating. When Asha carries on with her tests on the soil and the seed, a voice-over notifies her that she is conducting an "unauthorized" (Kahiu 2009: 07:31) test after which the council of three Black woman avatars appears on the screen before her. Being informed of Asha's findings, the traces of hope, curiosity, happiness, and distress are detectable in an instance on the faces of these avatars – and one may wonder whether the screen features actual human bodies or just a technologically generated illusion thereof. This, however, does not last long and the conversation is about to end when the woman in the front, who is – due to her center position and her habitus – assumed to have the highest rank, assertively notes: "the outside is dead." (Kahiu 2009: 07:51) Asha is being disqualified, however, she is adamant about her green vision and shares this future with them. Asha insists that "the soil is alive" (Kahiu 2009: 07:55) and, in order to prove it, she scans her hand next to the planted seed of Maitu. This way her visions are screened for the women – like avatars. Asha scans her hand as if she pledges solidarity to this future or in such a way that she holds this possibility in her hand. Followingly, one of the avatars reaches out with her hand to touch Asha's vision as if to partake in her dream and her alacrity. Yet the avatar-woman in the middle frowns upon it. Immediately, her hand slides on the image, in order to erase it. Hand, here, may symbolically serve to connote control, making, assistance, sharing, generosity, tactile sensation, communication, and the lack thereof. This is important in terms of answering for whom this future is preferable, who is willing to realize/hinder it, and why? For Asha, this potential is real, probable, and preferable not knowing that it is neither the matter of possible or probable for these avatars in power, rather the matter of preference, which precludes this future from being made. Put simply, when the position of those in power will be contested by alternate futureS, why lending a hand to make them happen. The clash between different sets of interests for the future and the subsequently different preferences seem to be the source of conflict in the shared now which also attests to the polyphony – or rather cacophony – in the notion of future.

Both "the council" of three avatars and later Denti leave Asha rather quickly. Maybe unbeknown to Asha, they plan to stop her. Yet Asha has for long desired such a future, somewhat echoing Bell claim that "the future depends on people's ability to judge preferable futures, to understand human values and goals that define conceptions of the good society" (Bell 1996a: 28). She begins to map her journey toward the future without hesitation and within the present setting and coordination. The scene in which Asha makes use of the compass and the map in the museum (Kahiu 2009: 09:14-07:13) to find the future's coordination is metonymically choreographed and it implies that the path towards the future begins from here and now and in continuation of ratios between past and present. And as such, any endeavor to delineate the correlation between past and present is, to some extent, about studying futureS.[3]

Herein, the music casts an auspicious quality over the narrative, a feature which thus far, except for the time that Asha encounters her dream in one of the early shots (Kahiu 2009: 00:51 – 01:14), was either barely audible, so as to render an un-naturally silenced and stifling feeling, or was mostly a monotone, minimal, electronic monophony to create an exaggerated feeling of

---

3 In this regard, Lasswell likewise notes: "Expectations about future may rest upon the extrapolation of past trends into the future." (1941: 456)

mechanical stagnation and digitalization. Music, antithetically with respect to former scenes, and harmonically linked to Asha's dream, frames the evolving of Maitu's seed; the pulse-like tone brings about a sense of living entity, suspense, hope, and ambivalence until it is precipitated by the invasion of the soldiers into the museum and completed by a deterrent shrill overtone.

5. Realizing the Preferable Future

Next thing, the security as represented by three Black men pours into the museum and destroys the remaining of other lives on the Earth (Kahiu 2009: 09:31-10:40). Asha is admonished; they arrest her, violently drag her out of the museum, and force her to be merely another body to generate power. Referring to the interrelation of present and the future, Bell asserts that "future thinking is largely about what to do now" (Bell 1996b: 11). Did other inhabitants of Maitu know about the possibility of life beyond Maitu is one thing, and if they have acted upon it, is another thing to be considered. Among those who did not share Asha's vision of a future, are those who feel endangered by it, those who do not desire it, the ignoramuses, i.e. those who did not know about it, because they had not ferreted out its possibility, or those who have never acted upon it. Amongst the latter, there is a white woman who serves as a maid. The same woman, who in one of the early shots, exchanges with Asha a look in the mirror – a glimpse of hope (Kahiu 2009: 03:10). The mirror symbolically stands for reflection and consequential patterns, not to mention the ample textual references within which a mirror portrays futureS. Back to the scene, Asha had responded with compassion and thus, donated some water to her. So, while cleaning the museum, after it has been ruined by the security staff, she dares to save Asha's dream by securing the compass. Perhaps she does not know about the future, yet she surely knows about hope and the power of being hopeful. She becomes the one to assist Asha, for she does not find the present likeable and therefore, does her "share" – in the language of Maitu community –, not to sustain, but to change it. With Asha's future, there comes the change for all living creatures of Maitu and beyond. Therefore, she hands Asha the compass and helps her to abscond Maitu with seed and the compass. In my reading, this semantic juxtaposition connotes that the path to futureS is furnished with hope, enlightened by collective consciousness, and achieved through collective agency. What separates Asha and the maid from the rest is the recognition of agency, future oriented decision-making, and then acing upon it regardless of its costs. This comes close to the point Bell makes on the history of science fiction and the transformation it has undergone: "Along with [some shifts in science fiction and utopian/dystopian thought, one] was that change toward a perfect world could be designed and directly brought about by human actions" (Bell 1996b: 4). What we see in this movie as a future scenario is not only the ways in which future is influenced by the choices, we make on a daily basis, but in addition, how with morally responsible actions and future thinking, as individuals and collectives, another, and a better future can emerge.

Asha, at the edge of dystopia, holds futureS in her hands and hopes to go beyond it, so as to gain freedom in a death that donates survival to futureS. In Bell's words: "[…] for an active person, the future is actually another dimension of freedom" (Bell 1996a: 43).

She leaves Maitu and enters the desert for a long march. There is still no water, there is still no life, but there is still Asha's hope as triggered by her dream. At the end of her long walk, Asha sees the tree she was looking for, but it is seemingly hardly more than a hallucination, however strong enough for her very last action in this life of hers: She plants the seed, watering it with her body's sweat, blood, and death. This reproduction of life queers any heteronormative idea of survival. For one thing it gives life via dying: Asha dedicates her life to realize her preferable future. She is alone and yet this is not a preferable future for her alone. Earth as well as all it contains are the shareholders of these futureS. For another, her queering futureS is based on a cross-species procreation of hum(pl)an(t). Asha dies by sacrificing her life to a seed, hosted by soil and her dreams. Together, they become a tree that is growing and thriving, becoming a forest and a future – and thus, she is the protagonist of futureS that ultimately equal nothing but the very present of ours – a present that offers water and trees, a present that is endangered by actions in Maitu's past. This is how "Pumzi" narrates a fascinating global ethics of and for future making; futureS that is for all and beyond segregations. Set side by side with Asha's death, possibly read as freedom, the nature is re-born; transcending lethal binaries such as human/nature and generating an understanding of un*animated human*nature that embraces technologies in due respect of the planet's needs.

The meaning of Maitu seed, which ironically is the name of the "techno-dictatorship", is worth pondering upon. In one of the opening shots it is captured what Maitu means: "MAITU (Mother) Seed". "Kikuyu Language. 1. Noun – Mother. Origin: Kikuyu Language from MAA (Truth) and ITU (Ours). Our Truth" (Kahiu 2009: 00:44). Building upon this premise that future is synonymous with *becoming*, and that Maitu seed is about to make different futureS, one can infer that "our truth" in "Pumzi" is laid in futureS, where the consequences of our today's actions are fully measured and realized. Having said that, and in the second layer of this irony, Maitu community is likewise "our truth" due to our current recklessness, irresponsibility, and passivity. Moreover, when "our truth" is being kept in a museum as (mere) past, and being regarded as a closed narrative, then "our truth" is castrated. Who we are is dependent on who we become and how we are is entangled with how others would be (then). Future is *becoming* and Maitu, a seed in yesterday, is a tree today and soon it becomes a forest (Kahiu 2009: 20:03) and a future. "Pumzi" therefore, narrates how a former impossibility morphs into a present possibility, an existing probability, and a future reality.

6. Incepting FutureS on Both Mind and Earth – A Concluding Remark

This article has delved into the literary representations, renegotiations, and entanglements of narrating futureS in "Pumzi". In so doing, Wendell Bell's account for future studies was deployed and translated as an analytical tool, in order to provide a systematic reading of the depictions and dialogues about futureS' visions. Having discerned the different levels of future, the representation of futureS in this brilliant Black science fiction was branched out into three types: (im)possible, (im)probable, and (un)preferable. And, in the final phase of analysis, the ratios and the entanglements of futureS were discussed.

Dealing with these issues, "Pumzi" is the labyrinth of futureS; it begins by opening a door to the future of human beings. The imaginative world of "Pumzi" is both where the future becomes the present and where the present makes futureS. By examining different doors which bring about varying futureS, and depicting the consequential conditions thereof, "Pumzi" narrates the art of navigating the future through futureS, and in a further step, advocates for posthumanist and holistic values for it.

"Pumzi" attests to the multiplicity of future precisely by depicting possible futureS for human beings, which can be overwritten by ferreting out other possibilities. In its imaginative literary world, "Pumzi" stages how visions for futureS of Asha, Maitu's elites, the white maid, and the Maitu seed may vary from each other in one single spacetime. For instance, Maitu's community is a probable future possibility – for the viewers – so is Asha's visions of a green future for Maitu community while stressing the unrivaled preferability of the latter. These are different layers of this labyrinth, which have their internal variations of future. Additionally, futureS are entangled; it is more about their entanglements and ratios than their existence. That is to say, future visions buttress, contest and/or annul each other. In "Pumzi", both the contrast and the compliment of futureS' visions are manifested. As policy makers in Maitu attempt to erase Asha's vision for future, in order to support their desirable futureS, the maid fortifies them. Yet, what makes the latter overcome the former is the deliberate decision making and acting with foresight as to realize and unite preferable futureS and avoid undesirable ones. Therefore, while futureS hold connections with past and the present, varying images of future must compete, survive, and can coexist.

That being said, the preferable images of future need to be disseminated, supported, and realized. And this is not limited to what's and whys. It is a major responsibility of futurists, based on Bell's account in "What Do We Mean by Future Studies?" (1996b) to "attempt to clarify goals and values, describe trends, explain conditions, formulate alternative images of the future, and invent, evaluate, and select policy alternatives" (10). Although to talk about future characteristics and predict probable scenarios are issues that can be the focus of all disciplines, it is merely through literature that one can imagine the incarnation thereof. Let us once again be reminded of the scene in which camera succinctly captures the harbingers of a doomed future and not least the human failure to stop it. This can be seized as a moment of realization that a literary narrative of future and its imaginative spheres are not all about transmitting facts and data but imagining how it is *really* like to live and/or to (re/un)make it. The ignorance of what could, or might, or will happen and what would be desirable for future generations might lead to not doing what would have been needed to hinder this future. Yet, what can stop undesirable futureS to happen are trained minds and imaginations, which are familiar with a broader spectrum of life and their respective desirabilities, meaning the alternatives of being – and an ethics of responsibility.

"Pumzi" allows us to go beyond binaries which are embedded in our world; and it is in this quality that the contribution of Black iconography to the field of futureS can be explored. It is very progressive how a deliberate decision is made in iconography of "Pumzi", in order to establish future aesthetics by moving beyond binaries. In "Pumzi", the future of Blacks and whites, women and men, nature and human are entangled and *evenly* affected. Noah Sow in her keynote held at the 41st African Literature Association Conference on "African Futures and Beyond. Visions in Transition" touches upon a noteworthy point which in my reading aligns with the poetics of the movie. On unchanging the imagination of Blacks for visions of future, she invites all to articulate their perspectives as "[…] a self-sustained source of empowerment; not a mere linkage to some established center but rather a center of its own." (Sow 2017: 28) Sow continues: "Intersectionality is Black.

Centralizing intersectional perspectives: the future of literature." (Sow 2017: 28) "Pumzi", in fact is promoting a liberating narrative of future while transcending the aesthetics of the contemporary, in which "the future is an open horizon that can be creatively explored" (Bell 1996a: 43), holistically assessed, and actively realized. Such a future is anchored at the intersection of meaning and matter, past, present, and future, dualities and pluralities, and facts and fiction. In "Pumzi", Asha depicts what is regarded as an *im*possibility, can be an existing possibility, and *becomes* the future.

Works Cited

Adam, Barbara. "Future Matters: Challenge for Social Theory and Social Inquiry." *Cultura e comunicazione* 1 (2010): 47-55.

Adam, Barbara; Groves, Chris. *Future Matters: Action, Knowledge, Ethics*. Leiden: Brill 2007.

Arndt, Susan. "Dream*hoping Memory into futureS, or: Reading Resistant Narratives about Maafa by Employing FutureS as a Critical Category of Analysis." *African Futures and Beyond. Visions in Transition*. Eds. Arndt, Susan; Ofuatey-Alazard, Nadja. *Journal of the African Literature Association* 11.1 (2017a): 3-27.

Arndt, Susan. "Human*Tree and the Un/Making of FutureS: A Posthumanist Reading of Wanrui Kahiu's Pumzi." *Future Scenarios of Global Cooperation – Practices and Challenges*. Eds. Dahlhaus, Nora; Weißkopf, Daniela. Duisburg: Käte Hamburger Kolleg 2017b: 127-136.

Bell, Wendell. "An Overview of Futures Studies." *The Knowledge Base of Future Studies*. Vol.1. Ed. Slaughter, Richard A. Hawthorn, Victoria, Australia: DDM Media Group 1996a: 28-56.

Bell, Wendell. "Choosing Your Future." *Viable Uptopian Ideas: Shaping a Better World*. Ed. Shostak, Arthur B. Armonk, N.Y: M.E. Sharpe 2003: 151-160.

Bell, Wendell. "What Do We Mean by Future Studies?" *New Thinking for a New Millennium*. Ed. Slaughter, Richard A. London: Routledge 1996b: 3-25.

Brubaker, Rogers; Cooper, Frederick. "Beyond 'Identity'." *Theory and Society* 29.1 (2000): 4-6.

Id. "Categories of Analysis and Categories of Practice. A Note on the Study of Muslims in European Countries of Immigration." *Ethnic and Racial Studies* 36.1 (2012): -8.

Gleick, Peter H. "Water Conflict Chronology." *Pacific Institute for Studies in Development, Environment, and Security* (Dec. 2015).

Kahiu, Wanuri (Director). *Pumzi*. Kenya 2009.

Lasswell, Harold D. "The Garrison State." *American Journal of Sociology* 46.4 (1941): 455-68.

Sow, Noah. "Diaspora Dynamics: Shaping the Future of Literature." *African Futures and Beyond. Visions in Transition*. Eds. Arndt, Susan; Ofuatey-Alazard, Nadja. *Journal of the African Literature Association* 11.1 (2017): 28-33.

TransSpecies Regeneration in Wanuri Kahiu's *Pumzi*[4]

Susan Arndt

European moralities have been largely pillared on a Manichaeism of nature versus culture, rendering culture as superior and hence entitled to tame nature. For one thing, this rhetoric positions animals, plants and inanimate materiality as nature as an antithesis to humans as culture. For another, humans themselves are subdivided along this very rhetoric, which can be traced back as far as antiquity.[5] Taking this thesis as its point of departure, this essay will explore the legacy of the nature-culture distinction in the context of the superior-inferior divide with regard to "being human". Thus framed, the article will make a plea for thinking beyond the concepts born of this divide, mobilising FutureS as a complementary category of analysis. This approach, in turn, will be utilised for a posthumanist reading of Wanuri Kahiu's "Pumzi" and its negotiation of agencies in the un/making of futureS.

1. The dead end of critical thinking – and beyond

Aristotle, for example, suggested that the Greek men were the only ones capable of practising reason, while Greek men can learn it, Greek women can only understand it. Those called, from the Greek racist perspective, "Barbarians"[6], however, were not even able to understand reason and hence could be used by the Greeks as means and tools (cf. Isaac 2004: 207-211). Discursively, this idea was fed into Christian narrations about difference (one need only consider Eve's punishment for wanting to taste the fruit of the tree of

---

4 My gratitude goes to Omid Soltani for his most careful and learned editing of the text and to Shirin Assa for very fruitful discussions about analysing the film.
5 For a detailed exploration of this rhetoric cf. Arndt, Susan. *Die 101 wichtigsten Fragen: Rassismus*. München: C.H. Beck, 2012.
6 The infamous term 'Barbarians' was initially used by the Greeks to other all those who did not speak Greek (not understanding their language, they would call them 'brr-brr sayers') and was later used as a homogenising label for all those who were not (considered) Greek.

knowledge) and was dis*continued throughout Medieval societal hierarchies right into the Renaissance and its humanism. Its celebration of human individuality strengthened anthropocentrism, which would set the human even more than before apart from nature. The Enlightenment again inhabited this rhetoric while adapting it, together with the notion of humanism, into contemporary findings and needs, on one hand, and equating reason with progress, on the other, thus suggesting that in the absence of reason there could be no progress, and vice versa. In doing so, the colonial space was positioned in what Dipesh Chakrabarty calls "not-yet" societies that were forever confined to the "waiting room of history" (2008: 9). Analogously, both People of Colour and women (Black women even more so than white women), amongst others, would be "not-yet" humans. In other words, in a linear conceptualisation of time, white Christian males were always ahead in terms of time and progress as compared to those they declared to be their "inferior Others". This European account of reason/intellect and progress is the gist of the matter in narratives that hold culture as antithetical to nature, suggesting: the more culture, the more human; the more nature, the less human. Throughout modernism and to date, this has rendered binarisms of gender, sexuality, religion, race, nation, class, and ability and the respective modes of discrimination all too well-known to this world – be it sexism, racism, classism, ableism, the discrimination against non-Christians, queer people etc.

The abovementioned pattern of "classification" according to underlying and multidimensional apparatus of discrimination has been generating power structures, respective epistemologies and social positions that have been practised and performed, affirmed and resisted, analysed and resituated in societal contexts, activism, arts and academia. Although today's offshoots of critical thinking – be it feminism, queerness, postcolonialism, Marxism or posthumanism – celebrate intersectionality, this classification still works within the linguistic legacy of the nature-versus-culture logic and its constructed criteria for scaling "being human". It is true; deconstruction employs a double movement of thought away from, for example, "race" or sex as a biologically constructed entity and towards *race* and gender as a social position (cf. Raman 1995: 255). Yet, by using these categories, critical thinking still gets mired linguistically and, thus, epistemologically in century-old powerful narrations of othering, as well as the very binarism of culture/nature that informs it, being translated into what Abdul JanMohamed calls the Manichean allegory "of good and evil, salvation and damnation, civilization and savagery, superiority and inferiority, intelligence and emotion, self and other, subject and object" (JanMohamed 1983: 4). The ongoing presence of this Manichean allegory, in turn, keeps forcing resistance into a rhetoric of defending the "othered" as is, for example, the case with Léopold Sédar Senghor's "Négritude" and Hélène Cixous's "écriture feminine" as celebration of Black or female emotion. Even though designed to subvert, the defensiveness at work here keeps powerful stereotypes alive. In due consequence, for critical thinking to be able to truly transgress given structures, discourses and epistemologies, it needs to think beyond the Manichean allegory of nature-versus-culture, its conceptualisations of difference and the rhetoric of defensiveness. Wary of this current aporia, this essay employs one of many possible categories of analysis capable of overcoming the Manichean rhetoric of securing power via othering: FutureS (cf. Arndt 2017).

2. FutureS as a Critical Category of Analysis

The "category of analysis", FutureS, interferes into "future" as a linear sequence of past, present and future and hence of progress. In doing so, it insists on three semantical pillars that induce me to speak of "futureS" rather than "the future". While having the capitalised "S" in common, the "F" is only capitalised (i.e. "FutureS") when referring to "the category of analysis", while "futureS" is my term for talking about the subject of "future" in a deconstructed way.[7]

Firstly, the capitalised S in both FutureS and futureS suggests that "future" does not exist in the (simplicity of any) singular. This very "S", *secondly*, draws attention to the fact that futureS are intersected and moulded by complexities and coexistences of "glocal" encounters of conflicting, competing and complementary agencies, interests, contingencies, possibilities and options in the un/making and (not) sharing of futureS. Throughout global histories, some futureS have buttressed each other, while some have deflated each other and others have prevented each other's existence; some have advanced and some hindered the other. There are futureS that neither did nor will ever happen, because one futurE thwarted the other – and in this instance, the capital "E" puts emphasis on this erasure of given pluralities. Consequently and *thirdly*, futureS (as moulded by and moulding the category of analysis "FutureS") are made and shared unevenly by power-coded agencies: "The future is already here, it's just not very evenly distributed", as internet visionary William Gibson (cf. 30.10.1999) suggests. Indeed, every struggle

---

[7] In due correspondence with the usage of "FutureS" as a category of analysis, I will use it (in terms of grammar) as *singularetantum*, while futureS as a pluralised term for talking *differently* about "future" keeps requiring the grammatical plural.

about power, freedom and justice is about futureS and every struggle about futureS is to strive for access to power, freedom and justice. After all, futureS' polyphony, complexity, reflexivity and relationality are coded by the structures and discourses of power, along the grammar of racialisation, gender, sexuality, religion, health, ability, age or nation. The social positions thus coded decide, to a high extent, about the very impact and agency a person or collective may have in shaping (their own and other people's) individual and collective futureS and their share of it. Ultimately, however, the struggle over futureS is not determined by power constellations alone. Rather, both power and futureS can be negotiated and un/made by agencies. Contextualised by power and powerlessness, privileges and deprivation, ethics and unscrupulousness, responsibility and the lack thereof, agencies desire and fear, fight and sustain, accept and negotiate, experience and forget, build and destroy futureS. In fact, agency is power's most virulent protagonist and antagonist at the same time.

Thus framed, in the following, FutureS will be mobilised as a category of analysis for a posthumanist rereading of fictionalisations of futureS as performed by (resistant) fictive and factual dreams and hopes and their power to procreate alternate futures. My argument will scrutinise the linear notion of time, reading past, present and future as being entangled in a cyclical causality: whatever has (not) happened keeps on affecting the present and its futureS. Moreover, I will discuss the intersection of memories, dreams and non*human agencies so as to demonstrate how they scrutinise the present and un/do this present's futureS. To put it simply, I will analyse non*human agencies that can affect the un/making of futureS and how the revisiting of the past (via memory) intersects with interventions into the present (via dreams) in the process. By way of example, I will discuss Wanuri Kahiu's short film *Pumzi* (Kahiu 2009), looking at its post-anthropocentric presentation of non*human agencies and the un/making of futureS in the interaction between technology and organic lives as well as the subsequent transgressing of the nature-culture divide and its binarisms.

3. Who is afraid of dreams in Wanuri Kahiu's "Pumzi"?

Wanuri Kahiu's "Pumzi" is set in an "East African Territory" 35 years after World War III, known as the "Water War", in a post-apocalyptic survival community called Maitu, which, as we learn, is a Kikuyu word meaning "Our Truth". Maitu's truth, as the film gradually reveals to us, is that the world outside is dead; an indoctrinated belief that has confined humans to life in this technology-governed habitat.

The opening high-angle shot of Maitu, resembling a brownish box in the midst of a wilderness, fades into newspaper clippings with headlines ranging from the all too familiar "Greenhouse Effect" to the more distressing "Whole day journey in search of water". These, together with the sight of skeletons and other remnants of dead animals as well as seeds stored in several jars, usher in the atmosphere of museum archives. The wide shot that follows introduces us to the protagonist, Asha, asleep at her desk, which faces a screen projecting some illusion of green life. A quick glimpse of her REM jump cuts into the dream itself, in which she, wearing a white dress with green patterns, appears full of joy and laughter, reaching for and flying towards a single green tree on top of a hill in the middle of a desert.

In the midst of her ecstasy, the foreboding, authoritative, siren-like voice of an electronic device is heard, incessantly warning "DREAM DETECTED" and commanding Asha: "Take your dream suppressants." (Kahiu 2009: 01:12-01:20). Awake, she lands back in her hi-tech surroundings, dressed in her dark khaki uniform, her blue eye shadow connecting the lifelessness of her conscious state to the lingering residue of her lively dreamscape. Obediently taking a pill, Asha is now wide awake, back in Maitu's reality.

Asha takes a bathroom break, walking us through what appears to be the cyclical routines of an ordinary day. She enters a hall with glassy walls that features Black men and women (skinny, yet in better physical shape than herself) cycling on fixed bikes. What seems to be a fitness centre at first soon turns out to be human bodies generating electric energy needed for Maitu's self-sustaining ecosystem. Upon passing a checkpoint, Asha is granted a daily dose of some 100 ml water. In the bathroom, she removes parts of her "armour", wiping the sweat off her body with a rag – which must pass as bathing in this environment – and wrings it into a container filled with her urine, which she then places in a recycling machine that turns those bodily fluids into drinkable water. Catching a cleaning woman's timid gaze, Asha shares some of her daily water ration with her, which suggests that water is a currency in Maitu and distributed unevenly among its inhabitants according to their social status. These two sequences familiarise us with Asha's own class, which as historian or archivist, is seemingly above the cleaning woman and the labouring bodies on bikes and treadmills.

The opening scene is reiterated and intensified when Asha returns to her office in the museum, passing the corpse of a tree, placed above a dated newspaper article featuring the picture of a tree under the heading: "There goes the last tree" (Kahiu 2009: 04:05). This header corresponds to the name of her workplace "Virtual Natural History Museum": the death of the very last tree represents the absence of non-human organic life in Maitu, which can only be accessed and remembered virtually and hence merely as an optical illusion and a bygone reality. This is at least what the museum keeps signifying: organic life cannot exist beyond the glassy walls of Maitu any more and Maitu is hence the last refuge for human life but at the expense of reducing "being human" to survival only.

This survival is, however, more about the illusion of being human than living. Various shots throughout the film feature human bodies at work, following orders. As is the case with dreams, emotions are generally suppressed, as are human interaction and communication. Intra-human communication being reduced to mimicry and watching each other, verbal communication takes place only in the realm of the digital and the virtual: the words that are heard belong to a voice-over that seems to merely translate the digitised communication in which the human body's only communicative movement is that of typing. Thus, verbal communication between human and technology is dominated by the latter's medium and governed by its language only.

The next sequence shows Asha holding a box "with no delivery note" (Kahiu 2009: 04:29); it has been addressed to her but in the place of a returning address it shows geographical coordinates. As soon as Asha begins to curiously examine the box, which contains a jar, she is asked by a virtual woman on a screen, named Denti: "Status report?" (Kahiu 2009: 04:19) Assuming that the box was sent by Denti, Asha reports that she will examine it; however, Denti denies being the sender and instructs Asha to report it to the security board (Kahiu 2009: 04:30-04:35). Rather than obeying her instructions, Asha starts the analysis and finds out that the soil in the jar (as diagnosed by a computer's voice) has "abnormally high water content" and "no radioactivity" (Kahiu 2009: 05:05-05:20). An understanding dawns on her that she will later put as: "[T]he soil is alive." (Kahiu 2009: 08:04) This is momentous news indeed, since it contradicts Maitu's "our truth" that animate life is impossible outside its container-world, thus making organic living within Maitu the sole "option" for human survival. Yet the reliability of this truth is now being questioned by Asha. In terms of age, she is too young to have ever known anything other than the post-WWIII Maitu. Yet, being the keeper of a virtual history of *natural* life, she is at home in the (hi) story of organic life and its death. This memory might be a crucial component to making her dream come true and envisioning alternate truths and futureS.

Upon touching and smelling this new soil for the very first time in her life, Asha falls back into her recurring dream (Kahiu 2009: 05:21-06:06) – a dream that was suppressed, yet did not stop in the wake of the museum's memories.

This time, however, the dream is not as gentle as in the previous one. Asha, once again wearing her green and white dress, falls into deep water, watching drowned roots of a tree while struggling to breathe. While she was smiling, indeed laughing in the first dream, now she seems to be horrified by the lack of oxygen. Nevertheless, this existential fear turns right into hope when Asha sees a tree bathed in sunlight, metaphorically referencing photosynthesis as the guarantee of human survival. A flashlight that might symbolise the aha-moment wakes her up in the double sense of the word: she stops fainting/dreaming, ready to cultivate her dream/agency in the soil.

The agencies of memory*dreams, soil and a seed prompt the protagonist Asha to insist on the possibility of alternate futureS (cf. Assa 2017), releasing a latent autonomy in Asha that makes her decide, somewhat hesitantly, to pursue the memory's dream-agency rather than taking a "dream suppressant". In doing so, she conceives a human*tree: she sows the dormant Mantis seed (that was seen stored in a glass jar in very early shots of the film), reunifying it with the soil and using her (body's) water, as partly recycled from her urine and sweat, to nourish it. The seed as a symbol of reproduction and potential futureS, takes its chance and agency, beginning to grow with rather supernatural rapidity. Insofar as Asha's name translates as "breath" in Kiswahili and as "hope" in Hindi, aptonymically we are facing a breath of hope: the hope that human beings can breathe oxygen as recycled from the carbon dioxide emanated by trees. "I am tasting its growth potential (...). This could mean (...) there is life on the outside" (Kahiu 2009: 06:55-07:05), says Asha. And while her words addressed to Denti still sound computer-animated, the growth potential of both the soil and her hope is featured by the background music that switches from electronic futurity to epic emotions and thus, iconographically, from technology to humanity.

This hope, however, is thwarted by Denti's "That is impossible" (Kahiu 2009: 07:06) and the consequent emergence of Maitu's body of governance, as represented by three Black women, on Asha's screen. They insist that "[t]he outside is dead" (Kahiu 2009: 07:53). Thus, rather than sharing Asha's hope that "the soil is alive" (Kahiu 2009: 07:54), the council asks Asha to take her pills, denies her request for an exit visa and insists on the nullity of her findings: "You are not qualified to determine that. Forward your work to science lab" (Kahiu 2009: 07:56-08:02). Thus, while the council privileges Maitu's "our truth" and those who confirm its technology-backed scientific evidence, Asha insists on the veracity of her own knowledge, revealed by the soil and the seed to her as the keeper of memory and the dreamer of alternate futures: "But I know it is alive. It has to be. Look!" (Kahiu 2009: 08:04-08:24) Asha scans her dream onto the screen and the council woman on the left seems to be tempted to reach for this dream, while the one on the right keeps closing her eyes. Yet the woman in the centre, standing a step ahead of the other two (and thus seemingly in the most powerful position) denies inspection by the others, ordering Asha again to take her dream suppressants and subsequently cancelling the communication. Denti reappears, only to withdraw her fragile solidarity completely (if there were any), rebuking Asha for having been compromised by her "ailment" since she stopped taking her medication: "I can't help you any more" (Kahiu 2009: 08:43-08:55). This 'any more' might again suggest that she *did* help her earlier and might even have been the one who sent Asha the soil in the first place, although now failing to be resistant enough to pursue the agency of dreaming towards alternate futureS.

Asha, in contrast, stops following orders; she grabs a compass, eager to map her route to the coordinates written on the box. Not long afterwards, three guardsmen barge in to destroy the museum and drag Asha out, transferring her to the hall of physical labourers, condemning her to toil alongside the same people we saw her passing by before – which might even suggest that some of them, too, might have been dissident ex-dreamers.

Obviously, the council of Maitu is afraid of Asha as empowered by the agency of the seed in the soil and her memory-driven dream, which are apparently stronger than that of the dream-suppressant pills. Therefore, the council decides to separate Asha from her memories (and their dreams) and the seed*soil: Yet why does the council feel endangered by this very alliance of the in*animate? Is the council representing human or organic interests at all? Or only those of technology? After all, who would be afraid of memories and dreams (of organic life outside of Maitu) – and why? Who gives the orders as represented by the computer voice and the council? Who would lose most when organic life is reborn of cross*species solidarity? Well, humans would not be harmed by the resurfacing of (dreams about) organic life at all, would they? Strictly speaking, technology would not be endangered either. Yet within Maitu, technology, that seems to be the only one speaking and giving orders, would lose control and power. So, in a nutshell, if technology is seemingly in control of Maitu and afraid of alternate (organic) futureS, are we not facing a techno-dictatorship in need of human labour to survive? Knowing that human labour can only be controlled if subjected to the illusion that the outside world is dead and that security and survival are only guaranteed within Maitu's utureogized habitat, eventually such a techno-dictatorship would be eager to suppress dreams and agencies for alternate futureS. According to this logic, the existence of the Mantis seed and its potential growing in the soil and thus Asha's memory-woven dreams are a significant menace to the techno-dictatorship, which (in their logic) needs to be eliminated. Therefore, the council needs to expel Asha from the museum to disconnect her from her memory, triggered by her dreams, as well as from the seed sown in the soil, as it cannot blossom without Asha's water and her dream-agency of finding a soil able to secure the seed's survival and its futureS as a forest.

Thus, the security that is apparently granted by Maitu is eventually dedicated to the established order of the techno-dictatorship only. Humans, in contrast, turn out to be exploited by it and eventually given hardly more than an illusion of some safety. Human obedience, as needed by the techno-dictatorship, is gained by complementing this illusion with the fear of death mixed with a mirage of freedom. In due correspondence, its walls of glass reinforce Maitu's illusion-based governance and its void promises of freedom and planetary belonging. Therefore, *true* organic *living* (beyond mere survival) and freedom and safety (beyond being imprisoned and exploited) can only be gained beyond the (b)orders and alleged security of Maitu's "our truth" – and it is found in "Pumzi", in a trans*species solidarity beyond its glassy gates.

About to give up the very agency to reach out beyond Maitu, Asha's earlier sharing of water with the white cleaning woman now returns to her as solidary agency. While Asha is dragged out of her memory, she insists on hoping and seemingly takes the seed with her, yet fails to secure the compass – which has, however, been pilfered by the cleaning woman. Telling her so by mere passing by, the dream and possibility of escaping towards futureS resurfaces in Asha: she flees to the outside with the fecundated soil, eager to plant the seed of her memory-woven dream*tree.

After a long bewildered march in a seemingly endless desert, Asha has (the aspired) hallucination of seeing a green tree. It is here that Asha plants the seed, nourishing it with the little drops of water left to her – and her body. The camera zooming out, her death is portrayed as the beginning of futureS of a cross*species recreation of organic life. The blossoming seed turns into a fragile human*plant that becomes a human*tree surrounded by the desert. The camera then pans out into an aerial shot depicting the fast-paced growth of the human*tree while a neighbouring rainforest seeps into the picture, turning desert-yellow into leaf-green, the whole uninterrupted sequence framed by letters spelling PUMZI.

Thus, ultimately, by donating her body across species and metamorphosing into a human*tree, Asha and other in*animate actors create futureS for planet earth that overcome the culture-nature divide and position humans in mutual entanglements (in terms of genes and conviviality) with other variants of organic life. In doing so, futureS here do not concern time and duration but becoming (true) at all – or remaining a truth, so to speak. After all, Asha will have arrived in a futurE that is synonymous with our present: a fragile and endangered environment. Asha's death as the beginning of futureS of a re-greened earth, able to provide water to organic life, is, ultimately, nothing but the state-of-the-art manifestation of this planet's situation – blue-green, alive and endangered. Thus, "Pumzi" intervenes into the present on behalf of futureS that need to be un/made before they can eventually happen: futureS that have to overcome the destruction of the planet, its water resources and all its in*organic entities by humans and their technologies.

Even if we do not know whether Asha's donation will endanger the techno-dictatorship in her world, for one thing, "Pumzi" suggests to *our* world that cross*species solidarity and responsibility beyond any culture-nature divide will generate alternate futureS most needed in the very now and for futureS. Moreover, dreams are narrated as agents of inspiration, imagination and intervention that offer opportunities that are beyond neither Asha's nor our own reach. Thus framed, dreams are narrated as the windows for alternate futureS, engaging the poetics of imagination in order to transcend reality. Just as Asha is a powerful actor because she dreams (virtual) memories, dreams are also generally one of the main sources of change and resistance against univocality, abused power and discrimination. They offer alternative scenarios and hence are powerful even when dedicated to unknown phenomena that cannot even be predicted yet. Dreams happen to become true, even if reached beyond one's own time by others and even by means that have not been envisioned yet (cf. Arndt 2017).

Secondly, "Pumzi" performs the overcoming of the nature-culture divide and its impact on conceptualising human beings and the times they inhabit. Rather than narrating time linearly and as progress, in "Pumzi" times are all entangled. While the film's overarching slowness puts emphasis on given continuities in cycles of power and oppression in a sense of "nothing ever changes", the ending happens eventually in an almost light speed sequence, thus putting emphasis on change. Yet, ultimately, the future thus screened intervenes into the present. In doing so, "Pumzi" narrates futureS as causal, i.e. as caused by the present and its past and the memory thereof, as well as reliant on cross*species interactions of responsibility beyond anthropocentrism and its history of classism, sexism or racism: Asha's expression of solidarity with the cleaning woman and the latter's subsequent reciprocation is just one side of the coin here; Asha profits from the agencies of dreams, the soil and a seed as well, but pays it forward by dedicating her life to organic life to thrive. On the other hand, the manifestation of their collective agency in saving the planet subverts the speculative tendency of mainstream works of fiction and sci-fi narratives that portray the (white) man as the only true saviour. In line with the discovery of the most ancient remnants of human presence on this planet (those of Lucy rather than Christianity's Eve) a Kenyan woman once again becomes the site of an origin narrative in "Pumzi" – a Kenyan film that hosts a Black woman's body, knowledge and memory-woven dreams as the backbone of a human*tree*soil agency towards alternate futureS beyond the nature-culture divide and its power-driven narrations about difference.

Works Cited

Arndt, Susan. *Die 101 wichtigsten Fragen: Rassismus.* München: C.H. Beck 2012.

Arndt, Susan. "Dream*hoping Memory into futureS, or: Reading Resistant Narratives about Maafa by Employing FutureS as a Critical Category of Analysis." *African Futures and Beyond. Visions in Transition.* Eds. Arndt, Susan; Ofuatey-Alazard, Nadja. *Journal of the African Literature Association* 11.1 (2017): 3-27.

Assa, Shirin. "*Pumzi*: The Labyrinth of FutureS." *Journal of the African Literature Association* 11.1 (2017): 58-69.

Isaac, Benjamin H. *The Invention of Racism in Classical Antiquity.* Princeton, NJ: Princeton University Press 2004.

Chakrabarty, Dipesh. *Provincializing Europe: Postcolonial Thought and Historical Difference.* Princeton, N. J.: Princeton University Press 2008.

Gibson, William. "The Science in Science Fiction." Interview. Audio blog post. *Talk of the Nation,* NPR 30.10.1999. http://www.npr.org/templates/story/story.php?storyId=1067220, accessed 01 February 2017.

Kahiu, Wanuri (Director). *Pumzi.* Kenya 2009.

JanMohamed, Abdul R. *Manichean Aesthetics. The Politics of Literature in Colonial Africa.* Amherst: University of Massachusetts Press 1983.

Raman, Shankar. "The Racial Turn: 'Race', Postkolonialität, Literaturwissenschaft." *Einführung in die Literaturwissenschaft.* Eds. Pechlivanos, Miltos; Rieger, Stefan; Struck, Wolfgang; Weitz, Michael. Berlin / Heidelberg: J.B. Metzler Verlag 1995: 241-255.

PUMZI – Eine filmische Gegenerinnerung der ökolonialen Gegenwart

Katrin Köppert

„Länder sind nicht arm, sie befinden sich nur in unterschiedlichen Zeitkapseln", schreibt Wanuri Kahiu in dem Band *African Futures* (Kahiu 2016). Sie nennt Beispiele: Simbabwe ist da, wo Kenia in den 1980er Jahren war, und Kenia ist, wo Südafrika 2000 war. Wenn ich Alexander Gauland (AfD) während des 2018er ZDF-Sommerinterviews zuhöre, dann – so scheint es – befindet sich Deutschland 2018 da, wo Kenia spätestens 2009 war. Gauland, der „glaubt", dass der CO_2-Ausstoß und die aktuelle Hitze in keinem Verhältnis zueinander stünden und der Mensch nichts tun könne, um das Klima zu beeinflussen (cf. ZDF 2018), können wir der Zeitlichkeit der Zu-spät-Gekommenen zurechnen. Das Bild des vom Westen reklamierten Fortschritts verkehrt sich in das des Ewig-Gestrigen. Wanuri Kahiu hingegen steht mit ihrem bereits 2009 erschienenen Science-Fiction-Kurzfilm „Pumzi" für ein Kenia, das in Anbetracht der Auswirkungen des Klimawandels längst schon realisiert hat, was die Zukunft birgt, wenn nicht jetzt Verantwortung übernommen wird. Dabei bringt der Film so geschickt Technologieaffinität und Naturverbundenheit in Einklang, dass man denken könnte, hier bräche eine Zukunft an, die gegenüber dem, was Kodwo Eshun „SF Capital" nennt (Eshun 2003: 290-292), gewappnet ist. Das heißt: Im Film, der die Zukunft Afrikas nicht nur mit Dystopie belegt, sondern durch die Agency einer Schwarzen Naturwissenschaftlerin, die zugleich Traumarchäologin ist, mit der Möglichkeit verbindet, Leben in der Postapokalypse entstehen zu lassen, haben wir es mit einer Science-Fiction-Narration zu tun, die nicht allein darauf ausgerichtet ist, die Kino- oder Netflix-Kassen durch die Vorausprogrammierung der Gegenwart klingeln zu lassen. Statt Zukunft als nur wenig zu Überraschungen neigende Ableitung von Gegenwart zu simulieren und zu kapitalisieren, entsteht eine alternative Zukunft, die auf Gegenerinnerungen beruht. Aber nun mal langsam. Die Zeilen wachsen gerade so schnell wie der Baum, der im Zentrum des Filmes steht.

1. *PUMZI*

35 Jahre nach dem Dritten Weltkrieg – dem sogenannten Wasser-Krieg – lebt eine autoritär organisierte Gesellschaft – die Maitu-Community – aufgrund der lebensbedrohlichen Hitze in einer überirdischen Kapsel inmitten einer kargen, nicht wirtlichen Wüstenlandschaft. Wasser ist knappe Ressource und wird nach einem strengen Sicherheitsablauf rationiert abgeben. Ein bestimmter Recycling-Apparat erlaubt es, den eigenen Urin und Schweiß in Trinkwasser umzuwandeln, das gleichzeitig als Währung fungiert. Strom wird schadstofffrei durch die Zwangsarbeit von auf Laufbändern arbeitenden Menschen erzeugt.

Asha – die tragende Protagonistin – ist Kuratorin des Virtual Natural History Museum und mit der Konservierung wie auch Erforschung der Rückstände eines Lebens beschäftigt, das ihr selbst unbekannt ist und nur durch Träume erscheint. Nach einem solchen Traum, der sie glücklich nach einem Baum greifend zeigt, erwacht Asha und findet nach Erledigung ihrer Morgentoilette ein ihr anonym zugesandtes Päckchen vor. Es enthält eine Erdprobe, die Asha sogleich und entgegen der Anweisung der per Hologramm zugeschalteten Vorgesetzten untersucht. Ihre Untersuchung ergibt, dass die Erde nicht radioaktiv verseucht ist und zudem einen außergewöhnlich hohen Wasseranteil aufweist. Die Riechprobe schließlich lässt sie in einen Traumschlaf sinken, der Bilder von ihr unter Wasser nach Luft ringend zeigt, während gleichzeitig Unterwasserwurzeln eines mächtigen Baumes zu sehen sind. Aufgeschreckt aus dem Traum entscheidet Asha, in die Erdprobe einen bereits archivierten Samen einzubringen und mit dem wenigen Wasser, das ihr für den Tag zur Verfügung steht, zu beträufeln. Vom Anblick erster Regungen aufgewühlt, flieht sie kurzentschlossen und entgegen des Verbots, die Kapsel zu verlassen, um den Keim einzupflanzen. Gegen die Brutalität der Sonne ankämpfend bahnt sich Asha einen Weg, lässt sich von der Fata Morgana eines Baumes inmitten der Wüste leiten, pflanzt das mittlerweile und wie in Zeitlupe gewachsene Bäumchen an die Stelle der Fata Morgana ein, um sich über den Hoffnungskeim wachend zu opfern. Asha stirbt, um – wie das Ende des Filmes vermuten lässt – einen Wald zum Leben erweckt zu haben.

2. Der Traum und/als das Undenkbare im Afrikanischen Futurismus

Was auf narrativer Ebene klassisch erzählt zu sein scheint, wird auf filmästhetischer, visueller und symbolischer Ebene mehrfach gebrochen. Der Traum spielt hierfür eine wesentliche Rolle.

Träume wie die von einem Leben mit Bäumen und Wasser sollen nach Maßgabe der regierenden Matriarchin der Maitu-Community mittels Sedativa unterdrückt werden. Während in „Inception" von Christopher Nolan (2010) der Traum zum Einfallstor der Manipulation von Menschen wird und somit als Waffe fungiert (vgl. Fitsch 2018), ist der Traum in „Pumzi" der auch ästhetisch artikulierte Katalysator des Subversiven. Das Leben mit Bäumen, das sich in das nur durch den Traum zum Vorschein kommende Unbewusste abgelagert hat, wird entgegen den sonst langsamen und ruhigen Einstellungen mit schnellen, pendelnden Kamerafahrten und Zooms dargestellt. Damit wird ein Sog erzeugt, der Asha ergreift bzw. von dem sich Asha entgegen der Direktive ergreifen lässt. Der Traum, der sie im Wasser nach Luft ringen lässt, ist Auslöser ihres Widerstands gegen das autoritäre und auf Überwachung und Kontrolle beruhende System. Aus diesem durch den Traum bedingten subversiven Akt entsteht schließlich die Realität neuen Lebens. Das Undenkbare, „was innerhalb des Spektrums möglicher Alternativen nicht begriffen werden kann, was alle Antworten auf den Kopf stellt, weil es die Begriffe untergräbt, in denen die Fragen formuliert werden" (Troillot 2002: 94)[8], erscheint aufgrund der Träume möglich.

Doch noch etwas Anderes ist an der zweiten Traumsequenz interessant. Ich würde sogar behaupten, dass sich in ihr die Positionierung Wanuri Kahius filmisch übersetzt. In ihrem 2014 veröffentlichten TED-Talk (cf. Kahiu 2014) argumentiert Kahiu, dass ihre Arbeiten nicht unbedingt dem Afrofuturismus zuzuordnen seien, weil diese Terminologie zu sehr mit der Diaspora verbunden sei. Eines der oft im Kontext diasporischen Afrofuturismus' genutzten Motive ist das der geschwächten oder bereits verstorbenen Schwarzen schwangeren Frau, die während des transatlantischen Sklavenhandels' über Bord geworfen wurde und deren unter Wasser geborene Kinder ein Schwarzes Atlantis gegründet haben (vgl. Diederichsen 1998: 109; Womack 2013: 87;). Dieser utopische Ort bildet neben dem Saturn eine wichtige afrofuturistische Topographie und wird – nach einer längeren Tradition der Aneignung durch Schwarze

---

8 Michel-Rolph Troillot bezieht sich hierbei auf das Undenkbare und trotzdem Erfolgreiche der Haitianischen Revolution.

männliche Künstler wie Sun Ra, Drexciya oder Underground Resistance – derzeit von vielen Schwarzen Künstlerinnen und Musikerinnern wie Aaliyah, Azeila Banks, Beyoncé, FKA Twigs uvm. adaptiert (vgl. Köppert 2017).

Kahiu nimmt das Motiv in der Traumsequenz auf, um es gleichzeitig zu verschieben. Die ins Wasser eintauchende Schwarze Frau scheint entgegen der Variante, in der die Kinder der Frauen in der Lage sind, unter Wasser zu atmen, keine Luft zu bekommen. Das Wasser wird nicht direkt zum utopischen Raum, der Traum nicht direkt das Fantastische. Eher entsteht das Unwahrscheinliche und Unerwartete in der Kopplung von Traum und Pragmatismus. Zwar rüttelt der Traum Asha auf, aber sie orientiert sich schließlich an den praktischen Abläufen einer Biologin, die aus der Beobachtung der Entwicklung von Leben entsprechende Schlüsse zieht. Insofern diese Schlüsse nicht nur rein erkenntnistheoretischer Natur sind, sondern praxisbezogener, erreicht Asha das kaum Denkbare, das für kaum noch für möglich Gehaltene: das Leben und Gedeihen eines Baumes.

Vielleicht ist es dies, was die Wendung oder Erweiterung des afrofuturistischen Motivs ausmacht: Nicht allein die Überwindung der Konträre *Science* und *Fiction* im Zusammenhang Schwarzer und afrikanischer Kultur scheint Kahiu zu interessieren, sondern eine Überwindung, die sich in eine konkrete und praxisbezogene Handlung übersetzt. Getragen von den traumhaften Geschichten und rationalen Handlungsabläufen naturwissenschaftlicher Forschung steht die Agency Schwarzer Weiblichkeit im Mittelpunkt, die Natur hervorbringt: nicht qua Natur, sondern durch Natur und deren auf Technologie beruhenden Methoden der Erzeugung und Erforschung.

3. Traumarchäologie: Das de/koloniale Naturkundemuseum

Kodwo Eshun schreibt am Anfang seines Artikels „Further Considerations on Afrofuturism": „Imagine a team of African archaeologists from the future (...) excavating a site, a museum from their past: a museum whose ruined documents and leaking discs are identifiable as belonging to our present, the early twenty-first century" (Eshun 2003: 287). Kahiu scheint dieses Vorstellungsbild filmisch übersetzt zu haben. Damit wäre sie nicht die erste, beruhen Eshuns Gedanken doch auf John Akomfrahs Film „The Last Angel of History" (1995). Jedoch wäre sie die erste, die filmisch eine Schwarze kenianische Frau in die Position der Archäologin aus der Zukunft versetzt, die mit den Restbeständen unserer Gegenwart ein Museum ihrer

Vergangenheit aufbaut. Dass dieses ein koloniales ist, ergibt sich aus dem Umstand, dass die ruinierten „Dokumente" der Natur, also die ausgetrockneten und radioaktiv verseuchten Überreste von Pflanzen und Tieren, Zeuginnen des neokolonial mitbedingten Klimawandels sind. Sie repräsentieren das durch neokoloniale Bedingungen geraubte Gut. Sind es heute naturkundliche Sammlungen, die – wie das dem Berliner Naturkundemuseum „gehörende" Skelett des Brachiosaurus brancai – zu verstehen geben, dass im Zusammenhang mit dem Kolonialismus naturkundliche Artefakte geraubt wurden (vgl. auch Zeller 2018), werden in der Zukunft Knochen, Skelette oder Pflanzenreste darauf verweisen, dass der Raubbau an der Natur heute unter neokolonialem Vorzeichen steht. Das heißt, dass die Kohleverbrennung, das Fahren von SUV-Autos, das Durchkreuzen der Meere mit Schweröl tankenden Luxusdampfern in einem kausalen Zusammenhang damit steht, dass der gesamte Kontinent Afrika bei einer Erderwärmung von 3-5 Grad noch in diesem Jahrhundert keine Landwirtschaft mehr wird betreiben können.

Was heißt das für die Dekolonialisierung der Museen der Zukunft? Der Traum – so meine Behauptung – spielt auch hierfür eine zentrale Rolle:

Im gleichen Atemzug, in dem Asha Dokumente archiviert, legt sie Träume frei und die mit diesen Träumen wiedererzählbaren Mythen. Der Mythos zum Beispiel von Gĩkũyũ und Mũmbi besagt, dass Ngai, der höchste Gott der ethnischen Gruppe der Kikuyu, Gĩkũyũ, dem von Ngai erschaffenen Stammesvater, das ihm gehörige Land zeigte und auf einen Feigenbaum wies. An dessen Stelle solle Gĩkũyũ seine Heimstätte gründen. Bei diesem Baum angelangt fand Gĩkũyũ Mũmbi, die Frau, mit der er neun Töchter haben sollte, die wiederum die neun Clans der Kikuyu gründeten. Asha, indem sie träumt, einen großen Baum aus weiter Ferne sehen und – durch digitale Bildebenenaufteilung und Zoom – nahezu ergreifen zu können, scheint den Mythos wiederzubeleben und gleichzeitig zu transformieren. Anstelle des Gründungsvaters Gĩkũyũ ist sie es, die den Baum erblickt, was – würden wir den Mythos weitdenken – zu einer lesbischen Konstellation führen könnte. Als Asha später im Film an die Stelle des Baumes gelangt, erscheint ihr jedoch keine Mũmbi verkörpernde Frau. Nur sie und ihr Baumwinzling bilden die „companian species" oder – wie Susan Arndt es ausdrückt – „cross*species interaction of responsibility beyond anthropocentrism" (Arndt 2017: 136). Aus der Vereinigung von Mensch und Pflanze entsteht schließlich das neue Leben. „Pumzi" suggeriert folglich, dass der Mensch – um es mit Donna Haraway auszudrücken (Haraway 2016) – Kompost geworden sein muss, um der Welt noch eine Chance zu geben.

Mythen, die sich im Kontext der Träume in die Museumsarbeit einfügen und sich gleichzeitig in Bezug auf Gender wie auch auf die Kategorie Mensch transformieren, bilden das dekoloniale Reservoir – das Virtuelle – des Virtual Natural History Museums. Um Restituierung wird es nicht mehr vordergründig gehen: Es wird kaum noch wer oder was da sein, der oder das restituiert werden könnte. Eher scheint das dekoloniale Museum der Zukunft darauf angewiesen zu sein, mit Natur, die nicht ist, durch Träume und Mythen zu interagieren. Daraus kann dann sogar ein Keim entstehen. Allerdings nur in Kenia, denn wenn die Gaulands weiter Politik betreiben, wird Deutschland nie dort angekommen sein, wo Wanuri Kahiu mit ihrem Film bereits 2009 war.

Works Cited

Arndt, Susan. "Human*Tree and the Un/Making of FutureS: A Posthumanist Reading of Wanrui Kahiu's *Pumzi*." *Future Scenarios of Global Cooperation - Practices and Challenges*. Ed. Dahlhaus, Nora; Weißkopf, Daniela. Duisburg: Käte Hamburger Kolleg 2017: 127-136.

Diederichsen, Diedrich. „Verloren unter Sternen. Das Mothership und andere Alternativen zur Erde und ihren Territorialien." *Loving the Alien. Science Fiction, Diaspora, Multikultur*. Ed. Diedrichsen, Diedrich. Berlin: ID-Verlag 1998: 104-133.

Eshun, Kodwo. "Further Considerations in Afrofuturism." *CR: The New Centennial Review* 3.2 (2003): 287-302.

Fitsch, Hannah. (2018): „Technische Dystopien und Utopien im Science Fiction." *Traum und Schlaf: Ein interdisziplinäres Handbuch*. Ed. Krovoza, Alfred; Walde, Christine. Stuttgart: J.B. Metzler: 116-119.

Haraway, Donna. *Staying with the Trouble. Making Kin in the Chthulucene*, Durham: Duke University Press 2016.

Kahiu, Wanuri. „Ahnen der Zukunft." *African Futures*. Eds. Heidenreich-Seleme, Lien; O'Toole, Sean. Bielefeld: Kerber 2016: 175-186.

Kahiu, Wanuri. "No more labels." *TEDxEuston* 04.02.2014. https://www.youtube.com/watch?v=4--BIlZE_78, accessed 31 August 2022.

Köppert, Katrin. „Glanz. Zur Diffraktion des Spiegels. Beyoncé und FKA twigs als ‚glänzende' Beispiele des ‚Schwarzwerdens'." *FKW//Zeitschrift für Geschlechterforschung und visuelle Kultur* 63 (2017): 49-54.

Troillot, Michel-Roplh. (2002) „Undenkbare Geschichte. Zur Bagatelisierung der haitischen Revolution." *Jenseits des Eurozentrismus. Postkoloniale Perspektiven in den Geschichts- und Kulturwissenschaften*. Eds. Conrad, Sebastian; Randeria, Shalini. Frankfurt am Main: Campus Verlag 2002: 84-115.

Womack, Ytasha. *Afrofuturism. The World of Black Sci-fi and Fantasy Culture.* Chicago: Chicago Reviewer Press 2013.

ZDF. „ZDF Sommerinterview mit Alexander Gauland (AfD)." *ZDF* 12.08.2018, https://www.youtube.com/watch?v=HWUvTqlbsjg, accessed 31 August 2022.

Zeller, Joachim (2018). „Postkolonialismus: Eine koloniale Schatzkammer." *iz3w - informationszentrum 3. Welt* 366 (2018).

Towards an Alternative Epistemology in *Pumzi*

Mingqing Yuan

Believing something is true doesn't make it true. But phenomena – whether lizards, electrons, or humans – exist only as a result of, and as part of, the world's ongoing intra-activity, its dynamic and contingent differentiation into specific relationalities. "We humans" don't make it so, not by dint of our own will, and not on our own. But through our advances, we participate in bringing forth the world in its specificity, including ourselves. We have to meet the universe halfway, to move toward what may come to be in ways that are accountable for our part in the world's differential becoming. All real living is meeting. And each meeting matters." (Barad 2007: 353)

1. Introduction

Posthumanism, as an emerging field, has raised doubt and challenges to the long existing division of nature and culture, human and animal, or reason and emotion since enlightenment and the advocate of humanism in western philosophy. Interestingly, quite often the understanding of posthumanism comes from posts Enlightenment thinkers like Derrida and Foucault, while thinkers like Fanon, Senghor or Wynter are still searching for their own humanism or voicing against the colonial discourse of relegating the colonized to subhumans. In this sense, posthumans runs a risk of "further denial of humanity to these same people", "when [they] have not been considered and treated as humans" (Shih 2012: 30). Then there might be a question occurring here: When we talk about posthumanism, which humanism or whose humanism do we mean?

In Xin Li's herein following article "Becoming the Tree – Ethico-Onto-Epistemological Configurations in Wanuri Kahiu's "Pumzi", the term "ethico-onto-epistemological" coined by Karen Barad is aimed to challenge the epistemology and ontology division generated in western philosophy, and to generate a turn in all three areas, ethics, ontology and epistemology. In her book „Meeting the Universe Halfway", Barad (2007) proposes the concept "intra-action", which "signifies the mutual constitution of entangled agencies" (33). However, this paper tries to interpret Wanuri Kahiu's movie as a turn from western epistemology to an alternative or African epistemology, such as proposed by Léopold Sédar Senghor, which also resists the human-centered humanism in western philosophy, the binary of self and other, and the division of epistemology and ontology. Even though Senghor is often criticized for repeating racial stereotypes or being nativist, his configuration of "dance the other" shares a similar conceptualization with Karen Barad's „intra-action", a similar distaste of the split of subject and object, and a similar reworking of relativity between human and non*human. Here Senghor and Barad are not placed in a comparative manner but adopted as complementary method to understand the specific context and implications of „Pumzi". Therefore, this paper attempts to read „Pumzi" not only as a current shift in western philosophy from humanism to posthumanism but also as a philosophical shift from western philosophy to African philosophy, which is doubtlessly with "a political charge" and "questions the self-image of philosophy as a prejudice-free, ahistorical form of knowledge" (Rettová 2016: 127-128).

2. Towards an Alternative Epistemology

From the very beginning of the movie, several shots show how the Third World War changes the environment with severe greenhouse effect and dead animal and plant bodies in the glass jar as biological specimen stored in the Virtual Natural History Museum. The seed in the glass jar is explained in language and tag below as "MAITU (mother) Seed: Kikuyu language 1. Noun – mother origin; Kikuyu language from MAA (truth) and ITU (Ours), our truth". Here it shows an overview of knowledge structure constructed through observation, dissection, and even destroying the object, and through language, defining, describing, delineating and classifying the object. The way to know the Other is through "the humanization of nature" or "domestication of nature" (Senghor; Kaal 1962: 3). Nature is stored, exhibited, labeled and archived in glass jars, separated from human and regulated, destroyed and conquered by human. This is where truth comes from and how it is constructed. In addition to the museum exhibition, an insurmountable gap between human and nature is also revealed in the separation between the technology dictated human living realm as shown with a shape of a cross and the nature or dessert which is depicted as inhabitable for human beings. To some extent, it implies that human is separate from nature and is better than nature since human still survives and thrives. If technology and this separation between human and nature can be interpreted as the result of modernity, the linear and theological development proposed by western philosophy in the colonial time, then Asha's dream and later action of going out are prominent symbols of challenge and resistance to colonial modernity and discourse of development, and of a search for an alternative "our truth" and a return to the land.

If the aim of African epistemology is "to recompose and reconstruct an autonomous and liberated African subjectivity [...] to establish an African theory of knowledge [...] reversing the effects of the cultural displacement brought about by colonialism" (Marzagora 2016: 161), then Asha's acts represent an escape from and resistance to techno-dictatorship, suppression of dream and denial of "our truth" and her return to the land; reunion with nature and commitment to the dream are clearly an attempt to shift to an African epistemology and to "an autonomous and liberated African subjectivity". When Asha receives the seed, what she does is to use laptop and technology to examine the seed on its location, origin, radioactivity and water content. The assessment of the seed points to a certain point and is set up as the destination for Asha when she goes out, but during her trip the compass is abandoned and her stop is not related to the destination of science research but to her dream, which is taken as an object to be suppressed by medicine produced by technology. To some extent, what Asha tries to do is not only to overcome the divide of nature and culture but also to escape the dominance of technology and modernity over "our truth". This is echoed with the end shot of a forest afar and the sound of thunderstorm which symbolizes the approaching of revolution and the possibility of deconstruction of Manichean division and realization of an epistemology beyond self and other. It is undeniable that Senghor has repeated the division and stereotyping, or even racism in his works, but his proposal of an alternative epistemology beyond the western one is not only philosophical but also political just as revealed in „Pumzi". What Asha deconstructs is not only the human and non*human division but also the seemingly "prejudice-free, ahistorical form of knowledge" (Rettová 2016: 128) generated from western philosophy. In this sense, Asha*Tree does not only create futureS (Arndt 2017) but also an attempt and a political engagement to search for an alternative and African epistemology, which is a meeting point of postcolonialism and posthumanism.

3. "Dance the Other" and Intra-action

It seems that Li's usage of becoming the tree entails a transformation of Asha into a tree and her arrival at being a tree as a final symbolisation of breaking and transcending human and non*human divide, which implies a human sacrifice or "donation" to the tree as an act of going beyond the Manichean allegory and Enlightenment humanism. However, does this human sacrifice or transformation really go beyond the focalization of human? Is there a direct link between the death of Asha and the birth of a tree? Or even, to be more provocative, is Asha's dream which initiates or inspires her act only a dream of her own in the very beginning? Only human can dream? This point A to point B, Asha becoming a/the tree, and the special emphasis on this becoming, indicates a separation of Asha and tree in the first place and a success of human will at last. I would like to delve into this implied causality between dream and Asha's act, between Asha and tree, to explore how Senghor's and Barad's concepts can be played out here.'

In Deleuze and Guattari's "Thousands of Plateaus", "a becoming lacks a subject distinct from itself; but also that it has no term, since its term in turn exists only as taken up in another becoming of which it is the subject, and which coexists, forms a block, with the first" (2005: 238). In this sense, becoming does not have a subject as a pre-existent entity, but is a subject in formation, in flux and in movement with the becoming process of it. And there is no object for a becoming to become in the end, unless in the situation of what Spivak claims to be "strategic essentialism" (cf. Spivak 1988). Becoming is open ended with multiplicity, constantly dynamic without arriving and stopping at a certain point, and no aim or object to achieve in the end. Accordingly, Asha and tree are entangled from the very beginning or even before their encounter in the material form and the intra-action between human and non*human is already taking place, since the tree is alive from the very beginning when Asha received it and its life is not achieved through Asha's sacrifice.

Meanwhile, the dream that Asha has with a green tree to be touched or within reach (Kahiu 2009: 01:06), can be understood not only as Asha's dream of the tree but also the dream of the tree or the seed, though it is represented through the dream of human being, which is rooted in Asha's memory and comes from her previous intra-action between Asha and tree. The entanglements or intra-action between Asha and the tree do not only start from the appearance of the seed on Asha's table, and the "transformation" or "transition" is not activated through Asha's death. Instead, the tree is within Asha and even vice versa. When Asha carries the tree to the desert, it can be understood as her meeting the universe halfway. It is in her agency that the tree seed is carried and being walked, but in the tree's perspective, the tree walks as well. To some extent, there should be no distinction of subject and object between Asha and tree; since they are relational. Just as Barad claims, "the line between subject and object is not fixed and it does not preexist particular practices of their engagement, but neither is it arbitrary. Rather, object and subject emerge through and as part of the specific nature of the material practices that are enacted" (Barad 2007: 359). Asha and tree are both becoming through the intra-action between them. This is also reflected in Senghor's formation that in contrast to Descartes' "I think, therefore I am", it should be "I feel, I dance the Other, I am" (Senghor 1962: 6). The distance between subject and object is dismissed, and the being is constructed through the "living the Other [...] to discover and to re-create, to identify oneself with the forces of life, to lead a fuller life" (Senghor 1962: 6).

In addition, the implication of Asha becoming a tree implies a logic of genetic or filial causality, or even reproduction in an exaggerate sense, which is not in the sense of Deleuze's sense of becoming, let alone the unexplained emphasis of Asha becoming a tree instead of becoming as an open-ended process. As Deleuze and Guattari (2005) state, "to become is not to progress or regress along a series. [...] [B]ecoming produces nothing other than itself. We fall into a false alternative if we say that you either imitate or you are. What is real is the becoming itself, the block of becoming, not the supposedly fixed terms through which that which becomes passes. [...] Becoming is always of a different order than filiation. It concerns alliance" (238). Thus, there is a risk in claiming Asha's becoming of a tree, since it might erase the creative, rhizomic relation between Asha and the tree and between Asha and all other non*human elements like water, soil, wind, sun and so on by claiming a linear death and life connection between Asha and tree. This is also implicated in Senghor's formulation of becoming that "he dies to himself to be reborn in the Other. He does not assimilate *it*, but himself. He does not take the Other's life, but strengthens his own with its life. For he lives a communal life with the Other, and in *sym-biosis* with it: he knows [and is thus born] it" (Senghor 1962: 6, italics in original). Death and rebirth do not symbolize a lineal or genetic inheritance from one to other but are an on-going becoming of an intra-activity between one and the other. It is not evolution or digression but coexisting, coexperiencing and coinhabiting in a communal becoming process.

4. Conclusion

It seems that there are overlapping between Senghor's advocate of "Dance the other" and Barad's conceptualization of "intra-action", which are both a shift and change in humanism of western philosophy and which entail a dynamic concept of becoming and a deconstruction of self and other. Therefore, "Pumzi" as a movie often situated in Afrofuturism is both a call for a shift to an alternative or African epistemology and a rethinking of human and non*human relations.

Works Cited

Arndt, Susan. "Human*Tree and the Un/Making of FutureS: A Posthumanist Reading of Wanrui Kahiu's *Pumzi*." *Future Scenarios of Global Cooperation - Practices and Challenges.* Ed. Dahlhaus, Nora; Weißkopf, Daniela. Duisburg: Käte Hamburger Kolleg 2017: 127-136.

Barad, Karen. *Meeting the Universe Halfway: Quantum Physics and the Entanglement of Matter and Meaning.* Durham, N.C.: Duke University Press 2007.

Deleuze, Gilles; Guattari, Félix. *A Thousand Plateaus: Capitalism and Schizophrenia.* Minneapolis: University of Minnesota Press 2005.

Kahiu, Wanuri (Director). *Pumzi.* Kenya 2009.

Marzagora, Sara. "The humanism of reconstruction: African intellectuals, decolonial critical theory and the opposition to the 'posts' (postmodernism, poststructuralism, postcolonialism)." *Journal of African Cultural Studies* 28.2 (2016): 161-178.

Rettová, Alena. "African Philosophy as a Radical Critique". *Journal of African Cultural Studies* 28.2 (2016): 127-131.

Senghor, Léopold Sédar; Kaal, H. "On Negrohood: Psychology of the African Negro." *Diogenes*, 10.37 (1962): 1–15.

Shih, Shu-mei. "Is the *Post* in Postsocialism the *Post* in Posthumanism?" *Social Text* 30.1 (2012): 27-50.

Spivak, Gayatri. 1988. "Can the Subaltern Speak?"
In Marxism and the Interpretation of Culture,
edited by Larry Grossberg and Cary Nelson,
66–111. Houndmills: Macmillan

Spivak, Gayatri. "Can the Subaltern Speak?" *Marxism and the Interpretation of Culture.* Eds. Grossberg, Larry; Nelson, Cary. Houndmills: Macmillan 1988: 66-111.

Becoming the Tree – Ethico-Onto-Epistemological Configurations in Wanuri Kahiu's *Pumzi*

Xin Li

1. Ethico-onto-epistemology: Being in Relation

The term ethico-onto-epistemology evokes critical thought within the framework of post-humanist discourses. Karen Barad, prominent scholar in posthumanist studies, coined the term to denote an entangled and relational dynamic that underlie the posthumanist ethics of relating to the other[9] (cf. 2003). Though coined by Barad within her own specific theoretical framework, the term, along with its potentiality for an ethical attitude toward the other, has come to represent a body of thinking that dates farther back than its nomenclature. It is a body of thinking that puts the ultimate dwelling of our being not in the closeness of the self, but in the relation with the other. Derrida, for example, follows Levinas' formulation of ethics in placing the relation with the other at the core of our being (cf. Derrida 1978; 1997). For him, there is no pure selfness nor pure otherness, they are always and already within each other – interdependent and inseparable. Deleuze and Guattari's ontology of becoming also speaks to this vision of relation. In „A Thousand Plateaus" (2004), they elaborate on the molecular nature of becoming, which, they argue, is nomadic, rhizomic, transversal and processual.

In this sense, they seek to challenge the traditional brand of ontology that has been sustained by dualistic values that stipulate a radical separation between things (matter/nature/other) and thoughts (human/culture/self), and the idea that things are bound by determinate and essential characteristics. Utilizing phenomena observed in quantum physics that contradicts such presumptions,[10] Barad (2007) illustrates the agential power of matter in the

---

9 The metaphysics of presence (via Derrida) construct the "other" as a binary opposition to the (human) self. Barad, along with other posthumanist theorists, seeks to challenge this notion by bringing relation into the understanding of our being.
10 In her book, Barad details the double-slit experiment in quantum physics, where electrons exhibit different characters under variable circumstances, to deconstruct and

shaping of knowledge and deconstructs the notion that knowledge and meaning (human/culture/self) exist independently of materiality (matter/nature/other). In Barad's agential realist ontology, or what she calls ethico-onto-epistemology, existing entities do not pre-exist their acting upon each other; their being emerges in an ecology of intra-action, or a web of relations. In other words, Barad, against the traditional ontology of being, proposes an onto-epistemology where the relation (intra-action) with the other precedes meaning and subjectivity – our being (human/culture/self) is defined by and situated in relation to and entanglement with the world (non*human/nature/other).[11]

Thus laid out, ethico-onto-epistemology encapsulates the formidable challenges that have been launched against the fundamental tenets of individualist metaphysics and the idea of "pure" presence (via Derrida 1978), and an emphasis on the agential power of matter in the shaping of meaning and knowledge. The ontological, epistemological and ethical turn toward the recognition of matter's constitutive power in the shaping of meaning and discursivity comprises the body of thoughts I draw on in my reading of "Pumzi".

"Pumzi" is a sci-fi short film written and directed by Kenyan filmmaker Wanuri Kahiu in the year 2009. The story is set 35 years after World War III, captioned as "the Water War" in an East African technocratic community called Maitu (meaning "Mother" or "OUR TRUTH" in Kikuyu language). Claiming that the world outside is dead, the authoritarian leadership of Maitu maintains its power and control on its people through a physical and onto-epistemological/ discursive separation between the human and the world outside its built environment. After receiving a mysterious bottle of soil that indicates the existence of life and an alternative to the dominant Maitu narrative/propaganda, Asha, the protagonist and curator at a Virtual Natural History Museum, fled from the protected habitat with the "Maitu (Mother) seed" (Kahiu 2009: 00:44) and took on an odyssey in search of life represented by a tree that recurrently appear in her dream-visions.

Susan Arndt, in her "Human*Tree and the Un/Making of FutureS: A Posthumanist Reading of Wanuri Kahiu's Pumzi" (2017), places agency in the soil, the seed, and the memory-driven dreaming of FutureS. For her, the main conflict in the film is set between the indoctrination of "Truth" and the

---

complicate the dualistic vision of being.
11 I use an asterik in between "non-" and "human" to highlight the point that the entanglement between the constructed "human" and "nonhuman" precedes the coming into being of any categories, identities or discourse. As to the specific use of the asterik, I draw my inspiration from my colleague James Wachira and his work in the field of posthumanism.

dream-agencies of alternative FutureS.[12] For me, though, the narrative dynamic is driven by an underlying strife of competing onto-epistemological presumptions – one between the oppositional and dualistic onto-epistemology of non-relation that dominates the Maitu discourse on "the outside" and the ethico-onto-epistemological entanglement of matter and meaning that culminates in the entangled life(/death) of Asha and the Mother seed.

2. The Outside is Dead: An Onto-epistemology of Dualism and Separation

The film begins with an aerial shot of a fort-like and futuristic architectural complex surrounded by a barren and abandoned landscape. The setting is already suggestive of the tension and dualism that dominates the Maitu discourse on the relation between the community and the outside world. The leadership of the community maintains its power through a fear rhetoric – they claim that "the outside is dead" (Kahiu 2009: 07:53), and the only way to survive is to isolate oneself within the walls of the fort, and against the threat of the outside. The oppositional positioning of the fort and its surroundings in the aerial shot forecasts the antagonism and separation in both its physical and discursive forms.

The dualistic outlook builds up in the following sequence, as the camera takes the audience through a "Virtual Natural History Museum" where nature(/the outside) is presented as a determinable object of knowledge (the archive), as well as an exterior and antagonistic entity. As the camera zooms in, the audience is presented with old newspaper clips and reports that portray nature in terms of degradation and intimidation to human survival. Water shortage, greenhouse effect, as well as narratives of human suffering (one article entitled "Whole day journey in search of water" features people who suffer from the lack of water (Kahiu 2009: 00:37)) are build and woven into a constructed opposition between the outside world and human existence within the controlled area of the Maitu community.

This outlook of separation/non-relation between the human and the non*human dominates the following sequence, where a ped-down shot

---

[12] I draw upon her theoretical configuration of FutureS/futureS in its relational and deconstructive understanding of constructed temporalities such as the past, the present and the future. She differentiates FutureS and futureS, the former a category of analysis that intervenes into the singular and linear understanding of future; the latter, a category of practice that highlights the future as a notion in becoming.

features a glass jar that contains a dry root of a plant with the word "DEAD" carved on it. It is followed by a close shot of a lifeless seed, the description of which reads "MAITU (Mother) Seed. [...] Kikuyu language from MAA (Truth) and ITU (Ours). OUR TRUTH" (Kahiu 2009: 00:44). The root and the seed featured in the sequence are material-symbolic instruments used to fuel the solidification of the "truth" that the leadership of the community upholds. The word "DEAD" carved on the glass jar is a footnote of such "truth" – it is a "truth" that subjugates nature to otherness and exteriority, a narrative constructed to instigate fear and maintain power. In this sense, the archiving of the root and seed, along with the rhetoric in the newspaper reports, put together a dualistic and antagonistic outlook that epitomizes the relation between the community and the world beyond its borders.

3. *Agency and Resistance: Entanglement of Matter and Meaning*

This outlook is challenged, though, by the materiality of a tree in Asha's dream visions, as well as that of an anonymous soil sample sent to her workplace. Immediately after the sequence that features the in*animate items in the museum, the camera moves on to the protagonist, who is sleeping on her desk. A detail shot of her closed eye takes her and the audience to the dream-vision of a green and full-grown tree amidst the vastness of wilderness. Asha smiles yearningly and stretches her hand toward the tree, but just before she is within touching distance, she is suddenly yanked out of her slumber by a robotic alarm sound that keeps repeating "Dream detected", commanding her to take her "dream suppressants" (Kahiu 2009: 01:13-01:19).

The tree in the dream vision is more than a product of the mind – for Asha, the tree is both real and physical (touchable) – the materiality of the tree is what triggers her desire to stretch out her arm toward it, as well as the longing that prompts Asha's eventual embrace of the vision it represents – a vision that challenges and contradicts the "truth" (that the outside is "DEAD") imposed (through panoptical devices such as the dream depressant) by the leadership of the community. Waking from her sleep, Asha starts to analyse the content of a package of soil addressed to her anonymously. Awed by the fact that the soil sample contains "abnormally high water content", "no radioactivity" (Kahiu 2009: 05:05-05:17), as well as the possibilities it represents, Asha spreads some of the soil on her own palm and takes a deep breath into her hand. The materiality (the smell, the touch, the moisture) of the soil triggers another instance of her dream-vision, in which she finds herself in a body of water, where she sees what resembles a cluster of floating tree root strands. Struggling and emerging out of the water, the vision of the same tree in the last dream flashes by before she wakes up.

Inspired by her dream-vision, Asha puts the lifeless Maitu (Mother) seed (presented in the last sequence) into the soil, along with her rationed water. As the dry seed regains its life and turnes into green, Asha is hardened in her faith in the existence of life outside the Maitu habitat. Planting the dry Maitu seed into the soil and observing its transformation from presumed death to promises of life, the protagonist becomes convinced in her long-simmering and alternative vision, which is given shape to by the agency of matters such as the seed, the soil, the tree, etc.. Confronted with the governing council's claim that the outside is dead, she retorts: "(T)he soil is alive…it must be!" (Kahiu 2009: 7:54-8:00). This is the first pronounced refutation of the dominant worldview purported by the leadership of the community, before it materialises into Asha's final act of resistance – of her escape from the fort in search for the origin of the soil, the matter that gives shape to the possibility of life, as well as the visions that dismantle the constructed narrative of death. In other words, the materiality of the soil, the seed, the tree and Asha's dream-visions grow with each other, feed into each other and get entangled in their agency of resistance and change.

4. *Toward an Ethico-onto-epistemology of Becoming*

This matter-vision materializes as Asha's journey ends with a symbolic/physical entanglement of human/tree, past/future, death/life. At the end of the film, Asha escapes from the enclosed habitat and takes on a long journey through a desert that seems to have no end in sight. Incapacitated by exhaustion, shortage of water and exposure to radiation, the protagonist falls to the ground and uses her remaining strength to plant the Maitu (Mother) seed in the soil, gives all the water she has left (body fluid or otherwise) to its nourishment, along with her own body. The camera zooms out into an aerial shot as Asha's body and the mother seed blossom into a human-tree-becoming, which expands to a long take that reveals a nearby and vast forest of human-tree-becomings that extends into a frame that spells "PUMZI", as well as the futureS the film envisions.

The materiality of the soil breathes life to Asha's depressed visions, which, in turn, led Asha to give her life for that of a human-tree-becoming. The moment of her presumed "death" is meshed with an emotional portrayal of life – in this scene, life and death, human and non*human are no longer separate and oppositional categories that dictate forms of human/non*human existence. Life continues, only in a different form – the body of Asha the human and the Maitu (mother) seed grow into a physical entanglement of life, which goes beyond dualistic prescriptions of life, death, and the divide between the human and the non*human. Asha's life is no longer contained in the closeness of an individual human body; it is now part of a larger entanglement of living and becoming that transcends the radical separation of the human and the non*human..

At the end of the scene, the zoom-out of the camera that reveals a nearby forest of human-tree-becomings gives no specified indication of its origin. Is the forest a recast of the past, or is it a vision of futureS? If the moment of the human-tree-becoming symbolizes the realization of possible futureS, the revelation of a nearby forest seems to indicate that the futureS are always and already part of the now. The slow and uninterrupted movement of the camera emanates a sense of motion and continuity, a symbolic gesture that mashes the present, the past and the futureS into one molecular time-becoming that defines every category in relation to another.

The seed and Asha's resistance exist in an entangled form of life, where both cannot live (materialize) without the other. In the film, the realization of Asha's visions is embodied in the fusion of the human and the non*human, an illustration of the ethico-onto-epistemological outlook that underlies the film's imagination of futureS, which appeals to an onto-epistemological interface between human and non*human agencies. Thus framed, the blossoming at the end of the film encapsulates the narrative dynamic where matter and meaning feed into each other, weaving an interrelated web of life, death and becoming.

This dynamic entails an onto-epistemological configuration that radically contradicts that presented in the beginning of the film – a configuration that sees materiality as a constitutive force in the shaping of our futureS. The discursive agency accorded to materialities such as the soil and the tree also entails an ethical attitude that appeals to the intertwined existence and wellbeing of the human and the non*human.

The envisioning of futureS in the film indicates a fundamental appeal to an onto-epistemology of becoming-the-world. Featuring the agency of matter in the shaping of meaning (futureS), the film intervenes into the anthropocentric ontology that dominates both the story world and our reality, which are always and already overlapping and acting upon each other. At a time when the materialities of water/air/greenhouse gasses shape the futureS of our world, the film points to an onto-epistemological vision that is neither antagonistic nor objectifying, but one that is ensconced in an ethics of relation and a call for responsibility.

Works Cited

Arndt, Susan. "Human*Tree and the Un/Making of FutureS: A Posthumanist Reading of Wanrui Kahiu's Pumzi." *Future Scenarios of Global Cooperation - Practices and Challenges*. Ed. Dahlhaus, Nora; Weißkopf, Daniela. Duisburg: Käte Hamburger Kolleg 2017: 127-136.

Barad, Karen. "Posthumanist Performativity: Toward an Understanding of How Matter Comes to Matter." *Signs: Journal of Women and Society* 28.3 (2003): 801-831.

Barad, Karen. *Meeting the Universe Halfway: Quantum Physics and the Entanglement of Matter and Meaning*. Durham, N.C.: Duke University Press 2007.

Deleuze, Gilles; Guattari, Félix. *A Thousand Plateaus: Capitalism and Schizophrenia*. London: Continuum 2004.

Derrida, Jacques. "Violence and Metaphysics." *Writing and Difference*. Ed. Derrida, Jacques. London: Routledge & Kegan Paul 1978: 70-153.

Derrida, Jacques. *Adieu to Emmanuel Levinas*. California: Stanford University Press 1997.

Kahiu, Wanuri (Director). *Pumzi*. Kenya 2009.

Becoming a Tree: Allegorizing Kenya's quests to save Mau Forest Complex in Wanuri Kahiu´s *Pumzi* (2009)

James Wachira

1. Introduction

This article reads the narrative in Wanuri Kahiu's *Pumzi* (2009) as a contemporary form of an allegory whose activism speaks to the seemingly incessant quests to save Kenya's Mau Forest Complex. Mau Forest Complex is among the five water towers in Kenya. The "Kenya Towers Agency" in its „Kenya Water Towers Status Report. Saving our Future & Heritage: A Call to Action" (2015) underlines the importance of the complex thus, "In the Mau complex alone, forests stretch over hills between the Rift Valley and Lake Victoria. It is source for twelve rivers that flow through the heart of Kenya. Its impact, through the rivers that flow into Lake Victoria, the source of the Nile, touches on the life of Egypt itself" (2). Therefore, the treatment of „Pumzi" as a framing of the quests to save Mau Forest Complex finds some explanation in Russell West-Pavlov's (2018) theory of aesthetics of proximity. The theory affords the article a definition of functions of Eastern African literature. In the analysis of the allegory, the tenet on the function of East African literature that applies in the analysis of „Pumzi" takes literature as, "the evocation of powerful forces of creative innovation emerging from indigenous traditions, from the natural and the built environments and from various forms of community forged in the face of socio-economic adversity and political stasis" (West Pavlov 2018: 4). The analysis deduces that the success of making the allegory lies in the strategic innovation of tapping into the "capital gains" in the phenomenal crowning of Wangari Maathai with the 2004 Nobel Peace Prize. The euphoria that the prize generated forged communities that, for instance, celebrated the first African woman winning the 2004 Nobel Peace Prize; the impact of Wangari Maathai in spearheading the Greenbelt Movement to list but a few. The communities in Kenya and beyond constitute, for this article, a structure that instantiates a series of networking with aspects of Afrofuturism culminating in the production of an allegory whose protagonist, Asha, a black female, is an embodiment of some of the ideals that define Wangari Maathai's environmentalism – exemplified in campaigns to save forests as well as in planting trees spanning more than three decades – as a means of petering out the dystopia that the Natural Virtual History Museum in "Pumzi" stands for.

2. Barad on Phenomena

In „Nature`s Queer Performativity" (2011), Barad defines phenomena, "as material entanglements enfolded and threaded through the *spacetimemattering* of the universe" (145-146). Barad`s conceptualisation/narration of phenomena, alludes to Niels Bohr`s 1913 model of the structure of the atom which builds on Max Planck`s 1900 constant. Bohr`s model is also a variant of Ernst Rutherford`s 1902 model on the possibility of elements to disintegrate and form other elements (Barad 2011: 136; Nobelprize 2018 Niels Bohr). For Barad, the significance of Bohr`s model in accounting for the structure of the atom as a kind of phenomena rests on the curiosity to find out if there is/are way(s) of telling the nature(s) of a phenomena that are detached from models employed in the speculation of phenomena. Barad (2011) arrives at the conclusion that the nature of phenomena exists as an entanglement and hence, "is inherently queer" (137). In proffering scientific modelling in accounting phenomena, Barad places the agency of queerity at the core of scientific speculations. In other words, the discovery is already "queer" considering that it is an investment to explore what lies beyond the boundaries of normativity. In Barad`s (2011) terms, models are, "materializing practices of differentiating" (124). It is in this light that I use „Pumzi" as a mode of knowing while at the same time, committing it as the prism with which I peek into Afrofuturism.

3. "Pumzi" and Afrofuturism

Afrofuturism entails, "re-readings of the past, negotiations of received stories, and establishing counter-histories to normative history" (Steinskog 2018:2). Steinskog (2018) adds that Afrofuturism`s dimensions include, "the speculative," the African* context, the relation to "technoculture," and the "prosthetically enhanced future" (3). Afrofuturism stresses that there cannot be a future without a past and, therefore, a comprehension of African futures is for Steinskog (2018), "simultaneously taking part in a conversation about history and time" (4). Therefore, an imagination of possible futures depends also on, "legible traces of black history, so as to be able to imagine possible futures" (Steinskog 2018: 4). Steinskog posits that Afrofuturism is obtainable from artworks. It is from this front that "Pumzi" waves onto the scene, as a model presenting possible futures. To explicate the presentations of futures, as phenomena in "Pumzi", I turn some attention to its sources, a *spacetimemattering* that materialises it as an Afrofuturist text, that includes oral sources, speculation, technoculture and a blend of dystopicism and hope.

4. Oral sources

Wanuri Kahiu in an interview argues that Afrofuturism predates the coining of the term. Singling out the employment of speculation in oral African narrations, one sifts some subtle admission of some influence of orality in "Pumzi". For instance, the title of the film could have derived from a popular song of „The Longombas", „Vuta Pumz[i]" that was a popular hit in the mid-2000s. „Vuta Pumzi" is Swahili for the conscious act of breathing in some air. The song stresses the possibility of getting HIV from the least expected sources. It as well offers tips on how to deal with the stigma of living with HIV. In the film, Asha, the protagonist on several occasions breathes in ways that arouse curiosity to understand her circumstances. For instance, in the first dream, she breathes in elation on seeing a tree. In the second dream, her swimming brings to the fore, her breathing evinced in the bubbling of water. In both occasions, the realization that she has been dreaming yields a different kind of breathing.

Another very common oral feature in the film is the journey motif. In the context of the film, Kahiu reworks the journey motif which in some oral narratives would be rendered in song or a chant. There are shots that capture the distance that Asha covers upon exiting the NHVM. The distance is presented with a trail of footprints, the wobbly walking of Asha that she punctuates with pauses, turns and peering into the horizons of landscapes behind and on the front. These acts summon both the past and future within her presence. Kahiu also subsumes both pasts and futures with(in) the naming of setting of the film, "maitu" community. In the film, the term "maitu" is defined in anthropocentric terms as meaning, our truth (human) or, mother. However, the term also transcends anthropocentrism when one considers its grammatical category as a possessive pronoun. As a possessive pronoun, it opens the possibility of considering futures for the Africans, black female Africans, nonhuman. Thus, upon its uttering, the name yields the three possible meanings.

5. Speculation

In the film, speculation is attained through dreaming as well as through the scientific experiments that Asha conducts at the NHVM. Both the dreaming and the scientific experiments yield epistemologies. The experiments in the NHVM represents human interaction with technocultures. The speculation in the film blends dystopicism with hope to present a human responseability that brings forth futures replete with environmental degradation and resource depletion and/or competition leading to wars over resources. Asha`s dreams and resolve to pursue her dreams is a form of activism that is seen as the hope for futures that cater for the needs of all. The ending of the film, with the letters that make the title of the film mimic a device through which we observe the universe. This is an anthropocentric positioning of presenting the universe.

Asha`s discovery of the soil with an abnormally high-water content and with no radioactivity likens to the LIGO discovery of gravitational waves and the horizons of knowledge they are expected to open (Nobelprize.org 2017). Asha`s discovery builds in her a curiosity to tell the source of the soil as well as to test its growth potential. Like Einstein`s prediction on the existence of gravitational waves, Asha is warned of the existence of a "dead" outside long before she is cast out of NHVM. Once out of the NHVM and then „Maitu", Asha walks through a wasteland where she experiences an environment littered with skeletons, choking in garbage, dried up rivers* (why do we call a dried river a river?), and no plants/trees seem to be growing. Asha`s resilience in search of the source of the soil with an abnormally high-water content and no radioactivity could also liken to the journeys in the advancement of LIGO to the extent it was able to observe gravitational waves. The excitement that observation of the gravitational waves elicits parallel Asha`s discovery that the mighty seed she had planted using the soil sample was growing (Nobelprize.org 2017). Thus, each model is an effort to what Michel Foucault terms a will to truth (cf. Sheridan 1980).

6. Wangari Maathai`s activism

"Pumzi" also bears the influence of Maathai`s activism on empowering women as well as on reforestation or protection of the environment. The award of the 2004 Nobel Peace Prize was a way of recognising her environmentalism/environmental justice efforts. "Pumzi" weaves Maathai`s concern with futurity. Maathai`s prism for materializing futures offers a disturbance, queers futures in way that resonates with Barad`s (2011) quantum erasure: "The past is not closed (it never was), but erasure (of all traces) is not what is at issue. The past is not present. 'Past' and 'future' are iteratively reconfigured and enfolded through the world's ongoing intra-activity. There is no inherently determinate relationship between past and future. Phenomena are not located in space and time; rather, phenomena are material entanglements" (145). On the one hand, it project(s) dystopicism supported embodied in the deforestation that „Pumzi" also finds (re)presentation in the film. The destruction of futures is also evident in the effort to make Asha be at home with her predefined role: "[Y]ou are not qualified to determine that." (Kahiu 2009: 07:56-08:02) The use of the pronoun YOU while addressing Asha serves the purpose of reminding her of her position as far as thinking of alternative futures are concerned. On the other hand, YOU in Baradian sense is a differentiating and a materializing apparatus. It is an affirmation of the agency of YOU in the constitution of an I. Asha`s pursuit of the source of the soil where she could plant the mighty seed is a metaphor for response-ability, the wave of activism toward environmental justice that characterized Wangari Maathai`s activism. "Pumzi" thus becomes a model for dis*abstracting environmental degradation through art such that the message and the urgency of pursuing environmental justice remains not a preserve of anointed races, disciplines, gender, class, nationalities and epistemological positions.

Conclusion

"Pumzi" demos that knowledge is not a given but a product that entails an entanglement of *spacetimemattering* as well as the apparatus at its disposal.

Works Cited

Barad, Karen. "Nature's Queer Performativity." *Qui Parle* 19.2 (2011): 121-158.
Kahiu, Wanuri (Director). *Pumzi*. Kenya 2009.
Kenya Towers Agency. *Kenya Water Towers Status Report. Saving our Future & Heritage: A Call to Action*. Nairobi: Kenya Towers Agency 2015.
Nobelprize.org. "Niels Bohr." *Nobelprize* 2018. www.nobelprize.org/nobel_prizes/physics/laureates/1922/bohr-facts.html, accessed 3 June 2018.
Nobelprize.org. "The Nobel Prize in Physics 2017 - Scientific background. The laser interferometer gravitational-wave observatory and the first direct observation of gravitational waves." *Nobelprize* 3.10.2017. www.nobelprize.org/nobel_prizes/physics/laureates/2017/advanced.html, accessed 4 June 2018.

Sheridan, Alan. *Michel Foucault. The Will to Truth*. London: Routledge 1980.
Steinskog, Erik. *Afrofuturism and Black Sound Studies. Culture, Technology, and Things to Come*. Cham: Palgrave Macmillan 2018.
West-Pavlov, Russell. *Eastern African Literatures. Towards an Aesthetics of Proximity*. Oxford: Oxford University Press 2018.

Signs of (and) Climate crisis: the Aesthetics of Wanuri Kahiu's Ecological Pedagogics in *Pumzi*

Oliver Nyambi

The term "crisis" has, in recent years, dominated discourses on climate change, global warming and the Anthropocene in local, regional and international debates on the future of human/nature relations. Crises denote, connote and imply states of distress when stressors destabilize and sometimes inhibit normative ways of seeing, comprehending and knowing certain phenomena. However, as recent biopolitical tensions playing out in global environmental, political and economic policy have shown, the ecological crisis does not merely entail the problematics of shifts in factors influencing regimes of knowledge, perceptions and interpretations of what environmental signs mean, what they will become and what (rea)actions they signify. Notions of the ecological crisis have accentuated aspects of its signs and causes that create or reinforce interested narratives of certain ecological realities. Science tells us that we live on a planet that is increasingly churning out signs with huge implications for how we live and (re)act vis-à-vis our sense of responsibility for sustaining a habitable earth for future generations. Whether it is "a climate of crisis" (Allit 2014: 1) or a "climate crisis" (Satgar 2018: 13) or both, one thing is clear; that we see and know the future of the earth from vantage points tainted by spatial and spatialized political, economic and psychological subjectivities. The question now is: what aspects of these subjectivities shape the ways we see, interpret and learn from ecological signs, and adjunct to that, what aspects of narratives and other forms of representations of these signs reflect, deepen and complicate what is known about the crisis and humanity's sense of responsibility for the future of the planet? In this chapter, I read Wanuri Kahiu's film „Pumzi" (2009) as an artistic example of narratives that subjectively emplot ecological signs to speculate about the future of environmental signs and create interested perceptions and meaning(s) of the state of human/nature relationship. My focus is on how Kahiu "reads" certain ecological signs and deploys her own system of narrative semiotics to aestheticize a certain view of such signs in ways that compel a specific understanding of humans' situation in the ecological future they predict.

"Pumzi" is part of an emerging corpus of African sci-fi adding to an already established genre of speculative fiction in Kenya in particular and Africa in general (cf. Yaszek 2006; Burnett 2015; Omelsky 2014). Although Kahiu has categorically denied deliberately intending the film to fit the category of sci-fi, a perfunctory look at the film's major themes reveal an ecological aesthetic that is reinforced through elements of plot structure, setting, discourse and symbolisms reminiscent of the genre. My concern in this paper is not with whether or not „Pumzi" adheres to any form of „standardized" modes of narrating sci-fi and/or speculative ecological fiction. Rather, my intention here is to find out how signs and (broadly speaking) symbolism are used as an integral part of narrative technique with implications for the aesthetic dimension to the film's ecological pedagogics. There are several symbolic signs that inform the film's environmental aesthetics. Depending on how one conceptualizes or frames "signs", of interest would be the Maitu seed, the heroine's dream and death, water, sweat, the desert, hue etc. These signs play a critical role in the film's narrative and aesthetic strategy for a pedagogic effect. They function as overt and covert enablers of plot, attracting and directing attention to a certain experience of the evoked crisis.

1. The crisis of signs

Much has been written about the nature, dynamics and functions of signs especially in theories and counter-theories of structuralism and post-structuralism (cf. Callinicos 1985; Zhang 2017; Givón 2016). At the heart of such debates is the dominant, yet often destabilized claim, particularly by structuralist theorists of text and narrative textuality, that the language of narration and the language in narration (including discourse) are essentially sign-systems that function more or less as mechanisms of signifying concepts and organizing meaning. Policy debates about the effects of human actions on the environment have invoked and accentuated specific signs in the present to create impressions of the human/nature condition that justify, in discursive ways, the need for certain (re)actions and not others. Whether it is the US-American president Donald Trump doubting the Anthropocene and resuscitating and raving up American fossil industries, Greta Thunberg, the Swedish girl leading school children in climate protests across Europe, or the Nobel laureate Wangari Maathai's "Green Belt Movement" fighting for social equity through sustainable use of resources in Kenya, signs are portrayed as sites of justification and argument for courses of actions with vested broader interests. Given the ontological and hermeneutic malleability, slipperiness and instability of signs in general, their signness, signage and signals are inherently unstable and prone to interested conceptions and usage especially in situations where (re)actions are needed. Environmental signs occupy a highly contested space in the unfolding debate on what kind of understanding of the state of the environment justify certain (in)actions. Although occurring in a shared world and proved by hard science, environmental signs are seen and felt differently depending on a range of factors. Such factors differently influence what facets of the signs matter to those who see and/or feel them. This means that although environmental signs are scientifically incontrovertible, they do not exist as arbitrary occurrences or forces that inform universal experiences, perceptions and understanding of their phenomenology. In fact, although the signs may occur universally, they are subjectively experienced, perceived, feared and acted upon. For people like Kahiu, Maathai and Thunberg whose experiences and perceptions of environmental signs have led them to pro-conservation initiatives, signs are not merely warning signals about what can go wrong if prevailing human/nature relations persist, but rather, what, whatever goes wrong, that would mean for humanity's capacity to sustain the ecological balance. This is not to imply that those not disposed to this kind of environmental concern are, of necessity, anti-nature. Rather, the difference in (re)actions to environmental signs between, say, the Trump administration's industrial policy and Kahiu, Maathai and Thunberg's activism, resides not only in their different experiences of the signs, but also in how their experiences inform their perceptions of what the future of such signs could become.

A necessary question at this juncture concerns what aspects of Kahiu's being in the present inform her futurist aesthetics and how her imagination of the future of environmental signs fundamentally differ from, say, Trump's. I am citing Trump here because his reactions to the same signs and interpretation of how their future should inform policy now reflects a radically different understanding and fear of the threat of futures signalled by environmental signs. When told that unrestricted global warming would adversely affect the USA economy in the near future, Trump replied: "I don't believe it."[13] (cited from Holden 2018) It is not immediately clear what Trump did (and does) not believe – it can be one or both of the two things: global warming and/or the negative impact of global warming on the country's economy. What is certain though, is that Trump's scepticism is related to his

---

13 Trump was responding to a report called the "National Climate Assessment" commissioned by his administration that predicted huge costs to the US-economy caused by climate change.

being a politician in a historical moment when fossil-driven industries make convenient short-term political sense for immediate campaign goals such as job provision. Concepts of the future signified by signs seen from different existential angles shape different forms of fear of the future of signs and drive both Kahiu and Trump into conflicting (re)actions. For Trump, the urge to deliver on political promises in the present, shapes his unbelief in environmental and economic futures that belie his industrial policy now. Contrastingly, Kahiu's environmentalism in „Pumzi" reveals an ethical disposition related to her fear of a future crisis.

2. The African gaze

It matters that the film is set in Africa, that it focalizes African experiences and must therefore be read as imagining African futures and their relationship to glocal environmental signs. This is not merely because centring African encounters and experiences of environmental signs provides an opportunity for Africa to converse with the world about a shared environmental future. Rather, the film's interest in African futures triggers the question of spatiality in considerations of how location influence unique experiences of the threat of environmental signs and trigger certain (re)actions to the fear of futures that such signs signify. Many aspects of situation, becoming and being a modern Africa influence uniquely African experiences of environmental signs, imaginings of what they will culminate into and how that imagined future culmination informs the kind of (re)actions needed now.

As many studies in the politics and economics of climate change have noted (Keohane 2015; Mahony; Hulme 2018), Africa's "underdevelopment" makes it especially susceptible to the vagaries of climate change and climate variation. Among many other factors, the stunted industrial base of most economies on the continent means that most people are still reliant on agriculture for survival. Agriculture is clearly at the mercy of severe shifts in climate and weather, and this means that signs of climate uncertainty easily translate into insecurities of yields and, indeed, futures. In „Pumzi" Kahiu spotlights these futures, showing us how their fatality must induce the fear of environmental signs, leading to a certain urgency in encumbering their teleological passage into a future crisis. This kind of urgency comes naturally to Kahiu, inter alia, because she inhabits a space whose fate is directly connected to climate. Kahiu's urgency to (re)act is informed by the fear of death and the threat of extinction. Unlike her, Trump's (in)actions, for instance, not only stem from the fear of being politically inconsistent but also from his impression that the resilience of US-America's diversified economy can either withstand future environmental crises or lessen the severity of climate-induced disasters.

3. Signs, symbols and the aesthetics of *Pumzi*'s ecological pedagogics

"Pumzi" is set in a post-apocalypse milieu where a small community of humans calling itself Maitu has invented and is experimenting with technology to help it harness whatever is left of the water on the planet to sustain life. It is 35 years after a World War III labelled the "Water War" that has left the earth uninhabitably dry, necessitating humans to artificially contain and regulate water in the secluded spaceship-like enclave. The Maitu community is essentially a high-tech hub where artificiality and science have not only replaced the natural world and environment but also substituted natural courses and processes of life involving water. Water is evoked as a symbolic resource undergoing equally symbolic artificial processes to sustain its existence and that of the war survivors. Water is therefore the most important symbol forming part of the signs that signify, define and characterise both the environmental and human conditions post the "Water War". Its signness, signal(s) and significations derive, for the most part, from its stable functions both in natural and artificial states and environments. The immediate question is: in what ways can we read water, particularly its various states, sources, and functions as a sign reflecting a state of future human existence related to (in)actions in the present?

Although reviewers of the film such as Durkin (2016) describe it as imagining an apocalyptic dystopia, the film, particularly in its ending, transcends this common feature of the ecological sci-fi. Without being overtly prescriptive, the film deploys signs – not to merely signal a pending environmental disaster, but more importantly, to reflect the necessity of human interventions in curbing signs propelling the planet to the disaster. Water is the major sign used to foreground the dystopian future of signs to illuminate the necessity of action now. Epitomized by the crisis of water shortage in the post-Water War Maitu community, the dystopian future in "Pumzi" provokes the fear of both the future and signs leading to it. This fear is aesthetically conjured and manifest subtly implied environmental ethics.

My notion of aesthetics here follows on the connection that Fiordo (1977) perceives between mediational functions of art and what he calls the "object value" (142) of signs. For Fiordo, although signs in art immediately link objects to value, they often do so mediately. He argues that "aesthetics includes both an immediate and a mediated taking account of value, which involves a work of art possessing both a sign-vehicle and its functioning as a sign" (Fiordo 1977: 142). In this view, the term "aesthetics" denotes and connotes the value of art as both a sign and medium of (and for) signs. To this Fiordo (1977) further adds: "[A]esthetics studies the valuative use of signs which signify goal-objects, with the additional requirement that the way signs are employed must awaken a positive valuation of themselves as goal-objects." (142) I have already indicated above that my reading of "Pumzi" views the film as a complex narrative "sign" that utilizes the sci-fi form to signify what can happen if certain human reactions to environmental signs do not happen in the present. In this functionalist sense, the narrative, which hints at what must happen to save the earth by foregrounding what happens in the future in the absence of interventions, can be viewed as an indexical sign in the strictest sense of the concept where the signifier is caused by the signified. As for "Pumzi", what is signified by environmental signs (a possible future environmental disaster) "causes", by way of necessitating, the sci-fi form. Through this form, an imagined future crisis is foregrounded as a sign in the future that, of necessity, must compel humans to take action about environmental signs in the present.

Reading "Pumzi" in light of Fiordo's (1977) notion of aesthetics as involving the "valuative use of signs which signify goal-objects" (142) raises the question: „whose values/goals"? Values and goals in "Pumzi" are intractably connected to both the sci-fi genre and how it is situated to perform an environmental pedagogic function. The film is set in a post-apocalyptic future when water has not only become a scarce resource but more importantly, has become a depleted force of enabling life. The film "valuates" the signness of water by foregrounding its symbolic uses as a source and enabler of life. We are introduced to the setting of the film through titles in white print on a black background. The titles date and locate the action as occurring in "Maitu Community, East African Territory: 35 years after World War III – 'The Water War'". In view of my focus on the aesthetics of the film's environmental pedagogics, perhaps the most important dimension to the characterization of the setting concerns how it portrays the future water crisis as resulting from environmental signs not acted upon. The question here is as to what is "pedagogic" about this setting and how can we read the state of water in the enclave as "teaching". In other words, to re-invoke Fiordo, what aspects of water palimpsested on its signness in its future occurrence "valuates" certain (inactions) associated with its past?

Ideas about the future of water shaped by encountering its crisis condition in the Maitu enclave engender the question of what could have been done to avert the future. In themselves, signs in the future Maitu community do not necessarily signify and/or compel a re-thinking of environmental protection in the present. What can potentially trigger the urge in viewers to save the environment is the extent to which the imagined future water crisis stemming from (in)actions in the present, incites fear. This kind of fear, I would like to argue, has its origins in what can be broadly termed human "conscience". There are several definitions and conceptions of what is meant by "conscience", each with often different if not conflicting implications for what drives human agency and urgencies in particular times and places. My own use of the term here borrows from Sinsawasdi's (2001) idea of "the inner feeling that tells people what is a good deed and what is a bad deed." (71) While Sinsawasdi makes a clear cut distinction between instinctive and learned behaviours, when viewed in light of the story in "Pumzi", "the feeling that encourages human beings to do good things and avoid doing bad things" (Sinsawasdi's 2001: 71) can be viewed as both instinctive and learned – instinctive because doing good (preserving the environment to save water) is a reaction to a life-threatening situation, and "learned" because that (re)action is urged by the fear of futures that is comprehended from the crisis situation necessitating the Maitu community. Sinsawasdi's example of conscience can explain the interwoven nature of "instinctive" and "learned" behaviours especially in cases where these actions concern perceived and real threats to life. He says that conscience entails "the awareness that stealing others' belongings is bad, and helping a drowning person is good" (Sinsawasdi 2001: 71). In this light and in relation to "Pumzi", we comprehend the goodness of acting on environmental warning signs now by imagining the water crisis in Maitu as resulting from our inactions. The future of water in the Maitu community not only incites the fear of human extinction which can potentially lead to what can be called an "environmental conscience", but more importantly, bridges the fictional and real lifeworlds in ways that elide hard boundaries in their realities and temporalities, making one a possible version of the other. In this light, the future Maitu community ceases to exist as a separate, surreal and unrelated world. Rather, its futurity connects with certain aspects of the present, real world to create a sense of what it can be if certain environmental actions are (not) taken.

Enhancing the viewer's seamless negotiation of the borderline between the imaginary future and her or his real world is key to the film's "valuative" construction of an environmental/water conscience. In collapsing the worldly border separating the future and present, the film allows the viewers to imagine the present as an earlier version of the future (and vice versa), thereby instilling, in the viewers, a sense of responsibility for what happens in the future. However, it is not a given that the viewers' imaginative self-situation in (and experience of) the future water crisis, of necessity, produces a keen sense of connectedness to it – a sense that this future, with all its dystopian realities, is something that they may live long enough to experience some day. In light of this complication of viewer response, Kahiu would have to count on the chance that viewers can, at least, relate to the humans experiencing the crisis. Barring, among other factors, the impulse for self-concern driving (as we have seen above) politicized economic/environmental policies, one can argue that encountering human suffering in the imagined future can potentially stir sympathetic emotions. As studies in the "intelligence of emotions" (Nussbaum 2001: 1) have shown, such emotions may not necessarily put the viewer in Asha's place and/or "circle of concern" (319), but they do connect her plight to a future dystopia that implicates the viewer through signs. This is because Asha's challenges in the future are connected to environmental warning signs within the viewer's capacity for intervention. Sympathy entails a sense of unjustified suffering. In "Pumzi", Asha's being an object of sympathy is connected to the fact that not only is she not responsible for her suffering – but also that her challenges are a result of inherited environmental situations stemming from the inactions of previous generations of humans – the generations of the viewers. This realisation of Asha's connectedness to us implicate us in her suffering and can potentially lead to an urge for self-introspection excited by our sense of guilt. If this feeling of guilt materialises, environmental conscience can kick in with no doubt as to what interventions in the present are needed to avert future environmental disasters of the kind suffered by Asha.

The Maitu community is a post-war community designed to be self-sufficient especially in the ways that it uses water and energy to sustain its existence outside natural systems destroyed by the World War III. The meanings and implications of the war culminating into this exclusive community have far-reaching consequences for the film's aesthetic mediation of environmental conservation. The World War III, also known as the "Water War", is the force behind the invention of the Maitu high-tech enclave where natural processes of obtaining, using, re-cycling and preserving water are technologically replaced. Perhaps the most basic implication of the World War III is the reality of an over-exploited environment getting too constrained by human actions to guarantee water. In this sense, the war is a metaphor for the future environmental crisis afflicting Asha's sci-fi world and is bound to happen in the real world of the viewer if humans do not change course vis-à-vis the prevailing human/nature relationship.

There are several discursive layers to the metaphorical and onomastic construction of the environmental crisis as both "World War III" and "Water War". "World War III" foregrounds the nomenclature of previous "man-made" crises (World Wars I and II) with global casualties to illustrate the spatial extent of the environmental crisis. The fear factor in the habitual collocative associations of 'war' is immediate. This fear, which inhabits correspondences of death, violence and pain typical of situations of war, is transferred to the crisis of water and, by implication, climate. The question, then, is as to what is feared and how does this object of fear and the nature of the fear it induces "valuate" (after Fiordo above) certain ways of seeing, comprehending, and knowing the war (read, "the climate crisis"). In other words, how can we read this fear as potentially aestheticizing the signness and signification of water for an environmental pedagogic effect; that is, in Fiordo's (1977) concept of aesthetics as "valuative use of signs which signify goal-objects" (142)?

As highlighted above, not all fears spring people into environmentally aware (re)actions and (as the Trump case above shows) not all threats of environmental crises induce fear. Fear necessitates (re)action when the feared object poses a threat to the existence of the fearing subject, thereby triggering the reactionary instinctive impulse for survival. In the Maitu community, the fear of extinction triggers technological inventions that preserve water through, among other methods, recycling human waste such as urine and sweat. These methods synchronize with popular "green" initiatives to save water in the viewer's world. The fear (with Asha), though, is that the Maitu initiatives are informed by a form of technological essentialism that impedes alternative approaches to mitigating the crisis. This essentialism best manifests in the Maitu Council's imperially dogmatic declaration that "the outside is dead" (Kahiu 2009: 07:51). This call forestalls interaction with the natural world and declines environment-minded people such as Asha the opportunity to save it.

However, although seemingly sustainable, the inside is not as enticing. Rico (2017) describes the Maitu enclave as a "sterile and inorganic post-apocalyptic compound" (89) where life inside the is monotonous, marked as it is by repetitive routines where members with solemn faces expend their energies on gym equipment that uses their kinetic energy to power the enclave. There is no social interaction and human conduct is guided by stern rules and punctuated with "mechanical" discourse. Social relationships are as unnatural as the enclave itself. Hue reinforces this flatness of life in the bunker. Virtually everything in the enclave is dark greyish, reflecting the vapidly insipid atmosphere, processes, relationships and work in the enclosed community. Further, this uninspiring ambience and the limiting tendencies it reflects manifest in the symbolic rationing of water. Members receive their share at a designated point where allocations are machine-coded under the watchful eye of grave-looking security guards. The process is strictly mechanical and all the three people involved in it only interact in a routine silent, robotic telepathy. While this highly formalized and policed system reflects a penchant for saving water and a deep understanding of its importance to human life, it also highlights how surveilled, constrained and constraining the methods of assuring its sustainability are.

What "valuates" the stifling of creativity and curtailing of alternatives to authorized modes of conserving water in the Maitu enclave is not the sheer sense of injustice manifest, for instance, in the Council's dictatorial authority over members' movements. Rather, the "valuation" occurs through the narrative's surreptitious emotional guidance of the viewer in recognising the enormity of a missed opportunity for rehabilitating the earth's environment when Asha, with practical, scientifically proven evidence of the outside's capacity for environmental rebirth, is denied exit to prove her findings by the Maitu Council governing the affairs of the enclave. As many studies in the psychology of emotions show (cf. Fredrickson 2003; Gergen 1995; Marcus 2000), emotions are at the centre of human cognition and action. Emotions result from the workings of feelings. This means that the viewers' emotional reaction to Asha's struggle with the Council and the authoritarian system it presides over is informed by how they feel – both about the Council's stranglehold over human interactions with the outside, and Asha's eventual resolution to defy the Council's embargo.

When Asha receives a mystery soil sample in her laboratory in the Virtual Natural History Museum inside the enclave, her tests suggest that the sample does not show any traces of radioactivity and that it contains a high moisture content atypical of a post-war wasteland planet certified by the Maitu Council as "dead". Upon this realisation, Asha applies for a "visa" to check the outside to confirm her findings, but she is swiftly denied permission by the heavy-handed Council. There is no apparent reason given by the Council for denying Asha's application for an exit visa except for the unsubstantiated claim that "the outside is dead." (Kahiu 2009: 07:51) The Council's irrationality is sharply contrasted with its ethical subversion by Asha whose intention to save the outside is portrayed as well-meaning and selfless. Asha's fear, which drives her resolute to disregard the Council's order has less to do with consequences for her intransigence – in any case her punishment would likely follow on her earlier penalty for testing the mysterious soil sample against the Council's orders to the contrary. In that instance, Asha is condemned to work-out in the gym where, besides undergoing a "healthy" rehabilitation exercise, her efforts generate energy for the enclave's proudly paraded "100% self power generation" project. Rather, Asha's fear which attracts viewers to her altruistic intentions is more connected to the potential loss of the opportunity to salvage whatever remains in the outside soil's capacity for re-vegetation.

Between the Council's fear that the outside is wasted beyond repair and the conscious viewers' own fear that the Council is mistaken stands Asha's dream of the lone, symbolic tree flourishing amidst a wasteland of dry, bare desert sand under scorching heat. The captivated viewer imaginatively occupies and identifies with the outside which shares much of what she or he can expect her/his planet to become if no (re)actions are taken to reverse the ongoing trail of environmental destruction. Now, to go back to Fiordo's conception of aesthetics and the question of what is "valued" vis-à-vis the film environmental pedagogics, it is important to note that the viewers' fear of the apocalyptic future that is imaginatively brought forward in time and represented as the outside of the Maitu enclave, informs a keen attachment to Asha's efforts to rehabilitate the planet. Asha's fear becomes the viewers'. It sprouts out of the suspicion that bureaucratic dictations suffocate hope, and that in the absence of opposition, whatever remains of the natural environment cannot be recovered and used as the launchpad for environmental regeneration.

As an environmental sign, the tree in Asha's dreams reflects several layers of meanings with deeper and sometimes conflicting implications for action. On one hand, the tree occurs in a dream and therefore, from the "scientific" gaze of the Council's rulebook, exists outside of what is remotely possible. In the essentialised world of hard sciences governing the Council's philosophy of the environmental crisis, dreams are not only scorned as unscientific, they are, in fact, catalogued as threats to the high-tech community hence their cataloguing for detection by the Maitu surveillance system. The seriousness of both their occurrence and perceived threat to the Maitu community is reflected in the use of the antidote – the "dream suppressants" to quash them. Thus when Asha enters into a dream trance where she finds herself in a large body of water and later on encountering a lone tree in the desert, she is immediately woken by a computerized voice announcing, in a holographic pitch, "dream detected", and instructing her to "take (her) dream suppressants" (Kahiu 2009: 01:12-01:20). Besides its censure as rationally implausible in the Maitu community's science-driven logic, Asha's dream is deemed a threat because its vision suggests a liberal epistemology that threatens the future of the enclave by vouching for a natural path to restoring the outside.

The tree in Asha's dream is not entirely a creation of her fantasy. Rather, the tree is a symbolic sign of the "green" future envisioned as possible if her resistance to essentialised epistemologies of the water crisis and physical containment in the enclave is successful. The "dream tree" demystifies and explodes boundaries of knowledge and worlds set by the Maitu community by envisaging greater and more desirable natural prospects for water and (implicitly) human life outside both the enclave and the artificiality of its "inside" knowledges and technological environment. Asha's "dream tree" is not totally illusory, at least in the form that it appears to her in her dream. When she decides to subvert the orders of the Council and steps out of the enclave to search for the tree and a place to grow the Maitu seedling sprouting from the outside soil she tested in the Museum, she gets disoriented from the vicious heat in the desolate land. In her confusion, she fancies the tree which appears to her in the form of an apparition. As she tries to embrace the tree, it vanishes, leaving her clutching on to the remains of a long dead tree cracking under the scorching desert sun. The powerful image of a mournful Asha embracing a desiccated tree where a thriving tree should have been and had been in her vision, reflects an undesirable state of the environment that not only gestures to the desirability of environmental revival but also suggests the possibility for regeneration – if only (and now that) she can dream. Here, the notion of dream transcends its normative conception by the Maitu Council as a mere imaginary world devoid of relevance to the pressing urgency of saving water and humanity. Rather, Asha's dream (the act) is driven by the object of her dream – the "dream tree" and what it symbolises – nature, growth and, indeed, water. In this light, we can read the "dream tree" as an imaginary "outside tree" that telepathically connects with (and summons) the real Maitu seedling sprouting under Asha's care inside the enclave.

The tree is therefore the Maitu seedling in Asha's future, thriving in an outside world that the Maitu Council has declared "dead". In this instance, dreaming extends beyond the mere subversion of bureaucratic epistemologies of the outside world, particularly what is known about its capacity for resuscitation. Dreaming here entails futurizing the present by imagining the future of the outside world (the desert) outside its known and normalized incapacity for re-vegetation. In this sense, the "dream tree" is essentially the future version of Asha's seedling from the enclave that has been brought forward in time to confirm its potential for growth in the condemned wasteland. The lush green and healthy tree thriving in the desert symbolises the possibility of a "green" future emerging from the wasteland. The likelihood of this dream future is evoked as guaranteed by the connection that Asha establishes between the "dream tree" and the Maitu seedling which makes the tree in the dream the future form of the real Maitu seedling she plants in the desert.

In "Pumzi", dreaming entails, among other things, transgressing the constraining authority of conveniently framed knowledges about the crisis state of the environment and the nature of possible mitigating measures. Asha's dream tree eventually materializes in the form of the grown Maitu tree and this makes dreaming a concrete ideal for dealing with the crisis. As Omelsky (2014) argues, thinking the "present-as-past through the optic of the future opens up the possibility of a restructured present and shift in the normative modes of social thought. It engenders a new politics of our historical moment" (48). To return to Fiordo's notion of aesthetics above, one can argue, with reference to the functional significance of dream and dreaming in "Pumzi" that what "valuates" Asha's dreaming is its capacity for turning impossibilities into realities. As the film ends, her intention to prove the outside's capacity for rehabilitation materialises when, upon confirming that the soil can still nurture plant life, she dies and becomes the source of nourishment for the seedling which mysteriously blossoms to become her "dream tree". Asha effectively becomes the sacrifice that triggers the collapse of the two previously antagonistic worlds (the enclave and the outside) as well as the distance in time between the Maitu seedling that she plants and the future "dream tree" that it mysteriously becomes.

The seedling becomes the tree that beckons rain. The tree, which is part human, is evoked as an ecological fetish with powers to summon rain. From a scientific perspective, the rain that immediately falls upon the tree's blossoming is nothing more than an indication of the successful re-balancing of the ecological system. However, a closer look at the rain, its nature and sources reveals signs and symbolisms that aesthetically signal and signify a broader story and discourse of environmental ethics in the age of intensifying anthropogenic crises of human-related environmental hazards. The rain is not merely a sign of a corrected, re-balanced ecosystem. Rather, tracing the rain's origins and occurrence, we can discern how certain aspects of its source (the human/plant combination) reveal pedagogic elements of its signness that reflect the ecological necessity of its preservation. In the closing scenes of the film, Asha's dead body gives life to the seedling which blossoms into a tree that in turn gives life to the barren desert.

4. Conclusion

As the film ends, the sound of rain can be heard over a mushrooming tropical forest not far from where the "Asha/tree" stands off Asha's remains. There is a clear cause-and-effect connection between the emergent forest, the rain and the "dream tree", that "valuates" becoming the "human*tree" (Arndt 2017) as an act of balancing the human/plant ecosystem. The events ending with a desirable outcome (the vegetation of the wasteland) is the culmination of a chain of processes beginning with Asha's "dream (of a) tree" and ending with her becoming part of the real tree that charms rain. Asha dies, both to give the tree life, and to live its life as part of the "human*tree". The rain and the forest are therefore identified – not with the tree but rather, the "human*tree" incorporating the tree's source of life – Asha. The growing tree consuming Asha's remains effectively makes her a part of its being in a way that vividly illuminates the possibility of a thriving planet given impetus when humans become interconnected with nature. Beyond it being a "human*tree", it is also a "teaching" tree. Its pedagogic significance can be felt in how Asha's transfiguration into a "human*tree" becomes an aesthetically didactic metaphor of life that gestures to its fulfilment when it becomes part of nature. Asha lives (in) her dream – the tree. She confirms its possibility (against the "science" culture of the Maitu enclave) by becoming part of its reality.

Works Cited

Allitt, Patrick (2014). *A Climate of Crisis: America in the Age of Environmentalism.* New York: Penguin 2014.

Arndt, Susan. "Human*Tree and the Un/Making of FutureS: A Posthumanist Reading of Wanrui Kahiu's *Pumzi*." *Future Scenarios of Global Cooperation - Practices and Challenges.* Ed. Dahlhaus, Nora; Weißkopf, Daniela. Duisburg: Käte Hamburger Kolleg 2017: 127-136.

Burnett, Joshua Yu."The great change and the great book: Nnedi Okorafor's postcolonial, post-apocalyptic Africa and the promise of black speculative fiction." *Research in African Literatures* 46.4 (2015): 133-150.

Callinicos, Alex. "Postmodernism, post-structuralism, post-Marxism?." *Theory, Culture & Society* 2.3 (1985): 85-101.

Durkin, Matthew. "Film Reviews: *Pumzi*." *African Studies Review*, 59.1 (2016): 230-232.

Fiordo, Richard A. *Charles Morris and the Criticism of Discourse.* Bloomington: Indiana University Press 1977.

Fredrickson, Barbara L. "The value of positive emotions: The emerging science of positive psychology is coming to understand why it's good to feel good." *American scientist* 91.4 (2003): 330-335.

Gergen, Kenneth J. "Metaphor and monophony in the 20th-century psychology of emotions." *History of the Human Sciences* 8.2 (1995): 1-23.

Givón, Talmy. "Beyond structuralism." *Studies in Language. International Journal sponsored by the Foundation "Foundations of Language"* 40.3 (2016): 681-704.

Holden, Emily. "Trump on own administration report: 'I don't believe it'." *The Guardian* 26.11.2018, https://www.theguardian.com/us-news/2018/nov/26/trump-national-climate-assessment-dont-believe, accessed 5 September 2022.

Kahiu, Wanuri (Director). *Pumzi.* Kenya 2009.

Keohane, Robert O. "The global politics of climate change: Challenge for political science." *PS: Political Science & Politics* 48.1 (2015): 19-26.

Mahony, Martin; Hulme, Mike. "Epistemic geographies of climate change: Science, space and politics." *Progress in Human Geography* 42.3 (2018): 395-424.

Marcus, George E. "Emotions in politics." *Annual review of political science* 3.1 (2000): 221-250.

Nussbaum, Martha C. *Upheavals of Thought: The Intelligence of Emotions.* Cambridge: Cambridge University Press 2001.

Omelsky, Matthew. "'After the End Times'. Postcrisis African Science Fiction." *Cambridge Journal of Postcolonial Literary Inquiry* 1.1 (2014): 33-49.

Rico, Amanda Renée. "Gendered ecologies and black feminist futures in Wanuri Kahiu's *Pumzi*, Wangechi Mutu's *The End of Eating Everything*, and Ibi Zoboi's "The farming of gods."" *Wagadu*, 18 (2017): 81-99.

Satgar, Vishwas. *The Climate Crisis. South African and global democratic eco-socialist alternatives.* Johannesburg: Wits University Press 2018.

Sinsawasdi, Narong. *Souls and the Universe: A Scientific Inquiry.* Bangkok: Oriental 2001.

Yaszek, Lisa. "Afrofuturism, science fiction, and the history of the future." *Socialism and Democracy* 20.3 (2006): 41-60.

Zhang, Shuping. "Meaning-Centrism in Roland Barthes' Structuralism." *Chinese Semiotic Studies* 13.3 (2017): 219-227.

Anti-dystopia, Afrofuturism and the Woman World: Re-thinking the Future in Wanuri Kahi'u's *Pumzi*

Dikko Muhammad

1. Introduction

As a science fiction film produced and directed by Kenyan Wanuri Kahi'u, "Pumzi" (2009) projects an alternative on how to imagine the future in a world of nuclear super powers and swift destruction of the climate. This film centers on what becomes of the world in the event of nuclear destruction; and how this dystopic end of the world can be faced and fought. This paper argues that "Pumzi" resists the urge to conform to the dystopian tradition of many science fiction, rather veering into an anti-dystopian direction. In doing so, it features agencies of change. Manifesting an African feminine imagination of the future, it revives hope for life, even when hope is lost and extinction seems inevitable. "Pumzi" philosophizes the future from a perspective that has not been given serious consideration. This is the sense in which Leonard (2003) has noted that "[S]cience fiction and the criticism of the genre have so far paid very little attention to the treatment of issues relating to race and ethnicity." (253) "Pumzi" presents the atmosphere on which the discourse of race and gender could be explored.

2. Science Fiction and Afrofuturism

This short science fiction movie, "Pumzi", opens with a setting described as the "Maitu Community. "MAITU (Mother) seed." "Kikuyu Language." 1. Noun- Mother. Origin: Kikuyu Language from MAA (Truth) and ITU (Ours). Our Truth." (Kahiu 2009: 00:44) This sign has Afro-futurist and feminist tendencies in it. In his attempt to explore the definitions of science fiction, Milner (2012) argues that: "SF [science fiction] cannot be located exclusively on either side of any high Literature/Popular culture binary, but should be seen as straddling and thereby, in effect, deconstructing them; that SF tends to be resistant to modernist aesthetics insofar as it privileges content, that is ideas, over form; and that SF narratives are typically tales of resonance and wonder, in which quasi-ideological resonance functions primarily so as to add plausibility to the tale's wondrous core" (22).

As a science fiction film that is ideologically laden, it is my contention that "Pumzi" falls within the above categorizations as outlined by Milner. Thus, it critiques contemporary issues that range from gender relations, environment destruction, to the impending dangers of political trivialization of nuclear issues by the superpowers. At this juncture, it is important to point out that "Pumzi" is not a fantastic display of linguistic aestheticism as the movie exhibits an aversion to spoken words. Hence, it fails to defamiliarize our consciousness of language. In fact, communication in "Pumzi" largely takes the form of facial expressions almost entirely, excluding the exchange between Asha, the museum curator of the community and the Council. Even here, the communication takes place on the template of modern technology because Asha types the messages and the Council speaks in the voice of a sentient computer. Even so, the technological advancement in the movie is most often a survival strategy than a display of adroitness of science and technology. In short, it is fairly easy to observe that in "Pumzi" technological advancement is subordinated to ideology.

In his critique of science fiction, Milner (2012) further engages the question on where to place it in academic studies. In an attempt to answer this question, Milner quotes Suvin (1979) who suggests that science fiction is, "(...) a literary genre whose necessary and sufficient conditions are the presence and interaction of estrangement and cognition, and whose formal device is an imaginative framework alternative to the author's empirical environment" (7-8). Unarguably, this definition inserts science fiction in the broader term of literature because it involves the literary-trinity of estrangement, formal devices and imagination. Needless to say, the threesomes are among the most notable characteristics of fictional works. This claim is supported by Eagleton (2007) who asserts that: "[...] when people at the moment call a piece literary, they generally have one of five things in mind, or some combination of them. They mean by 'literary' a work which is fictional, or which yields significant insight into human experience as opposed to reporting empirical truths, or which uses language in a peculiarly heightened, figurative or self-conscious way, or which is highly valued as a piece of writing." (25)

"Pumzi" fits perfectly into the category of the literary as defined by Eagleton (2007) above. In this regard, it is easy to fathom its fictionality through a power of invoking the reader's willing suspension of disbelief in addition to presenting issues and problems that are of great concern to humanity.

It is a narrative of the possibilities of what the future holds, not what absolutely lies in it. In fact, Pumzi's lack of heightened language does not entirely exclude it from the literary classification of Eagleton because he posits that possessing one of the five things mentioned is enough to qualify a work as literary. In spite of my earlier reservations about the movie's communicative competence, it could still be argued that its ingenious use of sentient computers as a medium for linguistic exchange is itself a heightened use of language that defamiliarises our perceptions of the world, in the sense Shlovsky describes it in his seminal essay "Art as Device" (1917/1919) (2016).

Similarly, Milner (2012) has argued that science fiction is literature because of its form, since "in traditional literary criticism, notions of 'form' or 'genre' are commonly used to classify literature and literary history (...) not by time or place (...) but by specifically literary types of organisation or structure" (35). He further stresses that even what we call literary is not strictly defined by the intrinsic features of such works. The decision is rather controlled and determined by certain factors and agencies. He posits that: "The 'literariness' of literature is not, in fact, a property of a certain type of writing but rather a function of how different kinds of writings are socially processed, by writers themselves and by readers, publishers, booksellers, literary critics and so on. What is defined canonically as Literature are, then, isolated examples of the actually or allegedly exceptional extracted from the wider context in which they were produced." (Milner 2012: 58).

Thus, going by Milner's argument, science fictions such as "Pumzi" are works that should be given the same attention as what we traditionally call literary works because they evolve almost through the same process of authorship, readerships and marketing. Moreover, it is their receptions by the viewing public that ultimately determine their place as canons or not. In addition, the academic study of such movies, especially in literary studies, will have an impact on their overall judgment including their profundity as works capable of receiving varied interpretations.

Sometimes science fictions like "Pumzi" does not feature a scenario that could be realistic. It is on this note that Shippey (2016) argues that science fiction, "creates an intense curiosity, as well as the pleasure of working out, in the long run, the logic underlying the author's decisions, vocabulary and invented world." (15) The viewer of "Pumzi" passes through this intense curiosity as it is a very short movie of twenty minutes. She keeps thinking of what would happen as Asha sets out in search of life. This makes the movie very suspenseful as the viewer keeps thinking of what will eventually happen to Asha and her living plant. Shippey insists that what we see in science fiction could not happen in the real world. He quotes Kingsley Amis' definition of the term that, "science fiction is that class of prose narrative treating of a situation that could not arise in the world we know, but which is hypothesised on the basis of some innovation in science or technology, or pseudo-science or pseudo-technology." (Shippey 2016: 15) However, what is more relevant is another definition quoted by Shippey (2016) that "science fiction is the search for a definition of (humanity) and (its) status in the universe which will stand in our advanced but confused state of knowledge." (15). This definition captures what "Pumzi" presents as a science fiction. In short, the movie is a definitive search for humanness.

Whether utopian or dystopian, the British literary and cultural critic, Raymond Williams (1988) cautions the outright dismissal of science fiction as a production outside what is considered as traditionally literary. He believes that science fiction is literary because it is a product of imagination. It is not made or observed. Thus, according to him, "[W]hen we look, then, at a contemporary phenomenon like SF [science fiction], we must be careful not to dismiss it because it is fanciful, extravagant, or even impossible, for, on the same limited grounds, we could dismiss *The Odyssey*, *The Tempest*, *Gulliver's Travels*, or *The Pilgrim's Progress*. The facts of SF are fictional, and can only be assessed in literary terms." (Williams 1988: 356). Thus, Williams equates science fiction with literary works because both involve the use of imagination and are fictional. He argues that to dismiss science fiction is to dismiss such classics as Homer and Shakespeare, and other highly celebrated authors. Williams argument on science fiction has contributed in the foregrounding and codification of the phenomenon in academic parlance. Ketterer, Rabkin and Baccolini (2005) support Williams' submission and compare the novel with science fiction and thereafter accord them same degree. They argue that, "for at least a couple of centuries, the novel and fiction generally have been accorded 'literary' value on the basis of realistic verisimilitude, the kind of science fiction (...) that is most highly valued by the literary and academic establishments is that of more realistic variety." (247) Panshin (1970) corroborates this stance and argues that science fiction is within the domain of literature because the progenitors of science are literary writers. He posits that: "If you define science fiction in the widest sense as stories of utopia and dystopia, of strange voyages and stranger places, it seems a remarkably reputable literary form. You might say, then, as science fiction historians have, that science fiction's ancestors were Plato, Lucian of Samosata, Sir Thomas More, Johannes Kepler, Cyrano de Bergerac, Jonathan Swift, Edgar Allen Poe, and always Verne and Wells" (884).

This is the sense in which "Pumzi" becomes interesting not just as science fiction, but also as production of postcolonial, feminist and eco-critical discourses. In his argument, Travis (2011), contends that, "science fiction has had a huge influence on the imagination of contemporary society, and most people are aware of its tropes from an early age." (243) As a genre, Travis argues that science fiction appeared in a magazine called *Amazing Stories* in 1926. The editor of the magazine, Hugo Gernsback, wrote that: "By 'scientification' I mean the Jules Verne, H.G Wells and Edgar Allen Poe type of story – a charming romance intermingled with scientific fact and prophetic vision (...). Not only do these amazing tales (...) [make] tremendously interesting reading – they are always instructive. They supply knowledge (...) in a very palatable form (...). New inventions pictured for us in the scientification of today are not at all impossible of realisation tomorrow. (quote from Travis 2011: 243)

3. Anti-dystopia through Dystopia in the World of Women

According to Claeys (2017), "the word dystopia evokes disturbing images (...) [it is] derived from two Greek words, *dus* and *topos*, meaning a diseased, bad, faulty, or unfavourable place." (3-4) On the surface, "Pumzi" strikes one as dystopian due to the horrible scenes in it and the seemingly hopelessness of its endings. However, as this chapter reiterates, in this seemingly dystopian movie, an anti-dystopian agenda is projected. The narrative privileges the continuity of life of other creatures on the planet even at the expense of the human one. The loss of Asha, the determined scientist in search of life, ensures human progression and averts the extinction of lives of the remaining people she has left at the enclave. Her quest to save humanity and the planet is not of a dystopian character/actress bent on a death-wish project. She follows her extinction to save lives, including that of her bossy superiors, who are not bold enough to venture outside, into the unknown in order to make connection between the destructive present and a future that awaits her sacrifice to blossom and be reborn. Thus, on this scale, "Pumzi" appears to produce an anti-dystopian narrative under the surface of its apparent dystopia. At the end of the trailer, the name, "PUMZI" appears with green shades and hope is restored again. "Pumzi" is not like the Orwellian "Nineteen Eighty Four's" (1949) dystopian future of hopelessness and anguish. In contrast, its future is full of optimism. It is highly optimistic that even when the world has lost everything, the fight for a cleaner environment is going to be won.

In this way, the world does not end. It undergoes a metamorphosis, a recurrent recycling of itself for another life cycle. It is like a phoenix; it rises and renews itself for another cycle, after an almost irrecoverable destruction. In this regard, when it goes near complete annihilation, the last among humanity will spark the process of reinventing and renewing itself, thereby subverting the dystopian narrative that the story seems to present on its surface. The world, like the soil and the plant in the hands of Asha, will continue to evolve itself and survive the tests of its inhabitants. Therefore, behind the obvious hopelessness and helplessness lie an irrepressible energy that defies all odds and ensures the ultimate survival of humans. This energy refuses to give in to telescreens, to acquiesce to the machos who storm the museum to destroy anything valuable in Asha's life-seeking project. Asha dares the warning that the outside is dead. In her we see that human desire, burning and unquenchable, for survival, for hope, the quest to explore possibilities and the undying hope even in the face of dicttaorship. "Pumzi" celebrates that hope to live even in the face of inevitable doom and destruction.

Often, science fiction comes as an admonition about what lies in the future, with scary details about the impending danger that resonates behind the discussions on global warming, the possibility of life in space and so on. This projection has been one of the earliest focal points that dominated the academic discussions of science fiction as argued by Tymn (1980) that one of the earlier studies of the genre, "gave direction to current criticism of science fiction by emphasizing its role as an important instrument of social diagnosis and warning." (220) However, "Pumzi" veers in another direction. It is certainly a warning about the danger that looms ahead, but it gives hope that the humanity will overcome the danger and the planet earth will be sanitized thereafter by the action of a woman, a (potential) "mother" who dissolves herself into nature and reincarnate into the "mother earth". Hence, "Pumzi" does not project a bleak future. It instead instills hope in humanity for a continued existence on planet earth. Ketterer, Rabkin and Baccolini (2005) have made the important observation that, "[M]any of the aliens of science fiction are best read as disguised representations of women or of oppressed races and classes." (247) This is in tandem with my argument that "Pumzi" projects Asha as a subaltern woman that sacrifices her life to save its co-inhabitants from extinction.

At the level of gender, "Pumzi" is a successful attempt to reinvent the female figure. It foregrounds the female first in the important role given to Asha, the female protagonist, amidst strong men. "Pumzi" unapologetically projects the future from the perspective of a "subaltern", African-woman film maker, in a movie industry unarguably dominated by white male producers.

It specifically privileges the experience of African women and uses Africa as its spatial setting. Here, African women, and Africans are given centre stage in the discourse of what awaits us in the future. In this regard, it is Asha who concentrates on the need to save the earth and humanity. She is not intimidated by the men. In fact, they appear to be intimidated by her presence as evidenced in the way one of them is disturbed by her presence. She is inquisitive, determined and the most intelligent of the team in the enclave. Where the other inhabitants of Maituu have accepted their condition of living a life without an assured future, Asha refuses to succumb to this boringly routine life, of physical exercise, and recycling of liquid waste. Instead, she continues her scientific experiment in search of life outside. She is a lean figure with a strong and sophisticated mind who debates the Council about the existence of life outside even when she is told that she is not in a position to decide that. In Asha, we see a determined and dissent future, not that of absolutism and dictatorship. Her portrayal gives hope that eventually, humanity will have a future that uses its own judgment, not succumbs to blind acceptance of the superiors.

"Pumzi" also glorifies the female sacrifice that paves the way for the continued existence of human generations and revival of the environment. Asha dies for the tree to grow and support life on the planet. Indeed, her end marks the return to the beginning of a green planet with rains, the default mode of the planet prior to fossilized human activities. It was a choice willingly taken in the guise of a woman sacrificing herself for the survival of her children. Asha is not frustrated by her quest for life outside. She does not die in vain. She carefully plants the seedling, nourish it with the remaining water that she ought to drink and strategically positions herself as a protective plank so as to facilitate the plant growth out of her decomposing body. This action is informed by the position of woman in the philosophy of many African cultures as argued by Mazrui (2004) that, "Africa has indeed expected its women sometimes to be ready to *die* for their people" (213, emphasis original). Asha leaves the comfort of the enclave in order to search for what would save the lives of generations to come.

4. The Composition and Power of the Council

Maitu Community, the spatial setting of "Pumzi", is governed by an all-female, powerful Council that dictates the running of its affairs. This is an interesting angle of the discourse about female power. This signifies the eventual taking over of control and decision making by women; perhaps after men have plunged the planet into destruction through the proliferation and use of nuclear warheads. In this Council, we see the concern for human lives as it denies Asha the required visa to go outside, as the outside is "dead" (Kahiu 2009: 07:51) and going out is tantamount to the death of a member of the species going extinct. Thus, Maitu appears to have learned its bitter lessons of male rule and has now turned to the female members to lead the community and save humanity from extinction. Nyawalo (2016) argues that "their seclusion from the outside world (...) gestures towards their inability to think or imagine an existence outside their immediate material realities" (217), unlike Asha whose determination is so strong that even dream depressants could not stop her from dreaming and hoping for salvation. Thus, it could be argued that "Pumzi" considers a future in which the humanity is tired of the destructive tendencies of men and displaces them, sending them into forced labor and enthroning the women to do the thinking and save the remaining members.

An interesting thing about Maitu community is that no woman is intimidated within its boundaries. Leadership is now both dictatorial and in the hands of women, even though majority of its members are male. As a corollary, "Pumzi" glorifies women and places hope that the future will be saved by women. It subsequently presents a coherent, systematic displacement of male authority and in its stead privileges female rule in the portrayal of Asha and The Council of Maitu community. It is a world where men are instruments of destruction (an example are the male members of the community that storm the museum and destroy Asha's research and discoveries) and women are invoked to safeguard lives including those of men that have reduced themselves to robotic activities. It is the intervention of the female bathroom attendant that saves the life of the little plant when the museum is invaded by the men who are determined to destroy every useful thing in it. Thus, the men in "Pumzi" are subordinated to the authority of the women. Even more, the responsibility of restoring life on the planet is placed firmly on the shoulders of the women.

5. "Pumzi" and Afro-futurist projects

Bowler (2017) argues that "futurology came into use in the 1950s to denote efforts to predict the future by extrapolating social and economic trends, increasingly via the use of computers to crunch the figures." (4) As an Afro-futurist production, "Pumzi" presents the world from the African perspective of determination, perseverance and faith in hope. The argument here is that "Pumzi", as a Kenyan production, is a science fiction different from many before it. Firstly, it privileges anti-dystopia in an apocalyptic setting. Secondly, it gives the African mind a vision of the future and spirit of holding onto hope and defying frustration. Thus, it could be argued that as a science fiction, "Pumzi" is a defying movie. It refuses to follow the tradition of its successors as it restores hope in humans in the face of obvious anarchy. This is the way that "Pumzi" shapes the discourse of the future. The African imagination in "Pumzi" refuses to conform to or follow the tradition of its successors. Thirdly, it provides an alternative to the way in which we speculate about future possibilities. It is interesting to stress here that it may not be surprising that "Pumzi" gives a positive future of the world since it is an African production. A continent that has witnessed the worst trauma in human history: slavery, imperialism, colonialism, and still suffers from the shackles and clutches of neo-colonialism in the form of theft of resources, both humans and natural, aid, debt and wars – but still clinging on to hope and refusing to be frustrated. This is so because, as "Pumzi" has demonstrated, there is success in the end of the story. It restores the hope that the humanity will continue to exist. Thus far, it is important to remember that in "Pumzi", the African continent is the fulcrum around which everything revolves. It is the origin from which everything originates from and to which everything refers to. It is a point of origin and an inevitable destination. It is the source where the human life originates and where the human species will be renewed in the desperate search for hope and survival. It is a place for a new beginning of humans and their environment when hopes are shattered and lives have perished. In essence, Africa is the last frontier in "Pumzi". The inscription referring to Kikuyu language is also a way of giving African invention a voice that is uniquely African, a voice denied to Africans in Shakespeare's "The Tempest", Defoe's "Robinson Crusoe" or Conrad's "Heart of Darkness" among many others. "Pumzi" demonstrates that Africa speaks many languages with which it can tell about itself. It is "MAA," the truth, and "TU", ours. The African language is not a borrowed language, neither is it a language of lies and propaganda. It is the language of the truth. It tells the African truth, the African invention and the African vision of life. "Pumzi" projects that the African continent is ready to tell its own version of truth in the discourse of science, environment, gender and the future of humanity. It demonstrates that Africa is no longer the silent, passive listener in discourses about humanity; it has its own perspective to tell in its own language.

In addition, "Pumzi" has an African fictional setting. It projects Africa as the last refuge for humanity when the world is contaminated by nuclear radiation. Here, the projection is tied to the specific idea of Africa being the origin of human beings and at the same time the last sanctuary of humanity in a dystopian, post-apocalypse world. The death of Asha, and her eventual decomposition that helps grow the plant into a thick forest signifies Africa's place in the future. Asha's ultimate sacrifice also portrays the humanity of a continent and a people still controlled by communalism and reverence for nature as the protector of the environment. The movie demonstrates that if there is hope for the future, with the nuclear race and the devastating wreckage of the environment by carbon emissions and other human activities, it lies in Africa. Africa is the origin where the story begins and where another chapter will open in the vast expense of human history.

On a political level, "Pumzi" could be seen as an admonition about the impending danger of nuclear proliferation by a continent that does not have nuclear warheads. "Pumzi" could also be seen as a warning about the aftermath of a nuclear war and the terrible conditions that human beings could face. In this reversal of roles in colonial adventure, it is Africa that now guides the world about what awaits humanity and human survival. This allows "Pumzi" to simulate the common tradition of science fiction as a warning about what approaches this planet and its inhabitants. This view is reflected by Bould and Vint (2011) who argue that, "science fictions are usually politically motivated and may directly exhort reader to work for social change so as to realise utopian wonders or avert dystopian terrors. SF emerged as a genre concerned with imagining the world otherwise and with constructing imaginary 'elsewheres' and 'elsewhens' in contrast to the known world." (20) The politics behind Pumzi is that of a continent that is no longer comfortable with suggestions by superior powers. It now admonishes these powers that their actions about nuclear radioactive materials could have severe consequences to humanity in general. "Pumzi" is a call for a nuclear-free planet. It tells about the doom, as well as the outcome of using nuclear weapons by those who possess them in a campaign to create a pacifist world. In general, "Pumzi" has achieved the status of science fiction through its presentation of an alternative future created by the imagination of an African woman. Leonard (2003) opines that, "science fiction writers can use its imaginative possibilities to hypothesize worlds where social problems have been solved; they can also imagine a future where the problems have been magnified or extended into a grim dystopia." (253) "Pumzi" presents a scenario in which the world undergoes rebirth through the sacrifice of a lone African woman.

Conclusion

"Pumzi" is a short science fiction film that redefines the identity and perception of the roles given to woman and projects Africa as a last refuge of human civilization. It calls attention to the African continent as the scientifically proven origin of humans and the final enclave of humanity in the face of impending dangers of global warming and nuclear proliferation. "Pumzi" achieves the task of redefining the African imagination and presents its perspective culturally, socially, and politically. Booker (1994) argues that, "(…) imaginative literature is one of the most important means by which any culture can investigate new ways of defining itself and of exploring alternatives to the social and political status quo." (3) This is what "Pumzi" has done in its presentation of alternatives to the socio-cultural and political crises of the modern world.

Works Cited

Booker, Keith M. *Dystopian Literature. A Theory and Research Guide.* London: Greenwood Press 1994.

Bould, Mark; Vint Sherryl. *The Routledge Concise History of Science Fiction.* London: Routledge 2011.

Bowler, Peter. *A History of the Future: Prophets of Progress from H.G Wells to Isaac Asimov.* Cambridge: Cambridge University Press 2017.

Butler, Christopher. "*Interpretation, Deconstruction and Ideology.* Oxford: Oxford University Press 1984.

Claeys, Gregory. *Dystopia: A Natural History.* Oxford: Oxford University Press 2017.

Eagleton, Terry. *How to Read a Poem.* Oxford: Blackwell 2007.

Kahiu, Wanuri (Director). *Pumzi.* Kenya 2009.

Ketterer, David; Rabkin, Eric; Baccolini, Raffaella. "Science Fiction and Imagination." *On Poetry* 120.1 (2005): 246-249.

Leonard, Elisabeth Anne. (2003) "Race and ethnicity in science fiction." *The Cambridge Companion to Science Fiction.* Eds. James, Edward; Mendleshon, Farah. Cambridge: Cambridge University Press 2003: 253-263.

Mazrui, Alamin M. "The Black Woman" *Race, Gender, and Culture Conflict: Debating the African Condition: Mazrui and His Critics.* Volume One. Eds. Mazrui, Alamin M.; Mutunga, Willy M. New Jersey: Africa World Pressm 2004: 211-252.

Milner, Andrew. *Locating Science Fiction.* Liverpool: Liverpool University Press 2012.

Nyawalo, Mich. "Afro-futurism and aesthetics of hope in Bekolo's *Les Saignantes* and Kahiu's *Pumzi.*" *Journal of African Literature Association* 2.10 (2016): 209-221.

Orwell, George. *Nineteen Eighty-Four.* London: Secker & Warburg 1949.

Panshin, Alexei. "Science Fiction Bibliography and Criticism." *American Libraries* 1.9 (1970): 884-885.

Shippey, Tom. *Hard Reading. Learning from Science Fiction.* Liverpool: Liverpool University Press 2016.

Shklovsky, Viktor. "Art as Device (1917/1919)." *Viktor Shklovsky. A Reader.* Ed. Berlina, Alexandra. New York et al.: Bloomsbury 2016: 73-96.

Suvin, Darko. *Metamorphoses of Science Fiction. On the Poetics and History of a Literary Genre.* New Haven: Yale University Press 1979

Travis, Mitchell. "Making Space: Law and Science Fiction." *Law and Literature* 23.2. (2011): 241-261.

Tymn, Marshall. "Masterpieces of Science-Fiction Criticism." *Mosaic: An Interdisciplinary Critical Journal* 13.3/4 (1980): 219-222.

Williams, Raymond. "Science Fiction." *Science Fiction Studies* 15.3 (1988): 356-360.

Blacks 'n Sci Fi

Raimi Gbadamosi

Outkast's 1996 album "ATLiens" shall be the soundtrack to this reading, when this paper becomes the blockbuster of a science-fiction film it is destined to be. This will happen when I am a hologram beaming in from another dimension. Not that Sun-Ra's "We Travel the Space Ways" (1967) has drifted from biologic-cybernetic memory as the man with another planet in mind, it is just that "ATLiens" rephrases the real world in its drift from the quotidian corruptions of blackness to convictions of complete difference to human beings. The inability to recognise the being in front of you is the real definition of alien, and by extension, alienation. So film will be scrutinised in preparation of this future moment eager to map futurity as blockbuster of Black agency – scrutinizing the silencing thereof in Hollywood blockbusters and awards. In doing so, the analysis will cross-read films such as "Logan's Run" (1976), "District 9" (2009) and "Chappie" (2015), "The Purge" (2013), "The Matrix" (1999), "The Hunger Games" (2012), "Independence Day" (1996) and "The World, the Flesh and the Devil" (1959).

The future is imagined each day, but socially and politically commodifiable visions backed by Capital are popularised on screens of differing sizes, as they capably yield economic returns, and foster population control. The importance of the screen as reality and metaphor cannot be overstated here, being that transfer of information/knowledge/interaction/data/innovation from all media to a screen interface (and by inference into a digitally retrievable form) has come to represent what the future will look like. So, the ability to sell the future today as part of a screen and screened existence is highly significant. Being that current and up-to-date access to the screen marks affinity with an acceptable future to the predetermined and intended audience, who see themselves as inheritors of any and all conceivable futures, screen-time itself places individuals in a future-present. The preponderance of screens-as-future is sometimes pushed to a radical edge within its redundancy as a virtual-reality (VR), three-dimensional, interactable object (a screen that can be walked into and be used, not to be conflated with the hologram.), but then again VR headsets already available to moneyed minority. The future is therefore being presented as a technicist utopia, where the current losers in the current technicism race will remain subservient to their wealthier counterparts, and as machines (smart or otherwise) replace the labour of the currently technologically challenged (which is a euphemism for a racially divided world, and this includes populations in the Global North), the emergence of the imagined racially exclusive future will make itself manifest.

1. Science in the Future in Fiction

Science-fiction allows the possibility of distance from the present. Hence, it is no surprise that the genre has supported the need for self-understanding against the backdrop of any now and its futures when living is hostile to global Black life. It is what A. Van Jordan points to in his poem "The Brother from Another Planet" (2012) with:

"Question: Do our shadows make us equals in light?
I'm an alien to those around me, though we
look alike ... They search my face ... They call me brother:
They say, "The brother has a way with machines, but he's short
on words." They say, "The brother just wants to sit in peace, man.
Leave him alone." But I want to stay among those who
call me *brother*, not left alone. I understand what they mean
when they talk, but I cannot *speak* their language;
I can only reply with my deeds. They seem to appreciate my honesty." (4)

Shadow and light – as core phrases of enlightenment they have contributed to treat Black lives with disrespect. Yet the lyrical I turns it, shadow is the centre, light the blueprint. This is why the I is considered to be an "alien to those around me"– *i.e.* not alien, but alienated: not as an alien, but as alienated. Paradoxically, this very "we" call the "I brother", making the I feel belonging to this "we" of "looking alike". But they call him "brother", but do not talk with the I – but about it. The lyrical I desires to converse, to belong – yet is left alone. Having a way "with machines" alludes to his being beyond geekiness: a cyborg or neural net processor. An honest one that does not speak but act; agency for unity in diversity in futurity.

The poem being made into an exceptional film of a continuing present, and space travel, by John Sayles ("The Brother from Another Planet" 1984), attests to the genre significance as a form of story-telling. Even if there is something in "the brother" (Joe Morton) going on to play Dr. Miles Bennett Dyson, the scientist who invented the neural net processor that eventually led to Skynet in the "Terminator" series (1984; 1991; 2003; 2009; 2015) that would threaten the destruction of mankind, only for humanity to be later saved by John Connor.

So science-fiction serves as a vehicle for imagining an alternative present, or any type of past or future that is desired, and whether what is imagined means divining a dystopia or utopia depends on a predefined point of view of what will best serve present interests. Richard Pryor (1989) describes a future in succinct reversal prose as presented in popular film. He said: "They had a movie of the future called *Logan's Run*. There ain't no n*ggers in it. I said, 'Well, white folks ain't planning for us to be here. That's why we got to make movies. But we got to make some really hip movies. Not movies about pimps. We done made enough movies about pimps, because white folks already know about pimping.'" (Bicentennial N*gger: 15:51)[*14]

Yes, every time I watch a Hollywood Blockbuster, they make Black people die. Africa drowns first and Africanist characters (in the sense of Morrison 2015) are but the pawn sacrifice in catastrophes solved and survived by whites only. So, whose futures, for whom?

2. Exclusion in the Future

The limitations placed on Black people and Black bodies in science-fiction films, demands that one questions the role of Black people in science fiction narratives, when the presence of blackness causes pause for all readers of written and filmed texts.

To assume that Black people do not simply perform a role in science-fiction films beyond characterisation is to assume the lack of willingness to cast Black people in film roles. Is this owed to the assumption as when a science-fiction film is made that the future, the world featured in science-fiction has managed to expunge racism and prejudice, because it deals with worlds concerned with real- or pseudo-scientific invention? Or is it just the longevity of white supremacy and its "evasion of race" (Morrison 2015: 64), or "myth of sameness", to use bell hooks' (2015: 167) wording?

But then all popular fiction films are fictional abstractions, and the casting of Black actors has not improved, the number of leading roles has not increased. In this it is hard to forget Chris Rock's monologue at the 88th Annual Academy Awards, if only because it was so funny to me watching people laugh nervously at the absurdity of a complaint that was not going to

---

14 editors note: Because we can't know for sure if the n-word here is used in an empowered reclaiming way, we've decided to edit it // edition assemblage

be addressed by the people being embarrassed. Chris Rock said: "Well I'm here at the Academy Awards. Otherwise known as the White People's Choice Awards. You realize, if they nominated host, I wouldn't even get this job! Y'all would be watching Neil Patrick Harris right now. But here's the crazy thing. This is the wildest, craziest Oscars to ever host because we got all this controversy – no black nominees. And people are like. 'Chris, you should boycott! Chris, you should quit! You should quit.' How come it's only unemployed people that tell you to quit something, you know? No one with a job ever tells you to quit. So I thought about quitting. I thought about it real hard, but I realized, 'They're gonna have the Oscars anyway'" (quote from: Fallon 2017).

Of course, white supremacy keeps casting white characters, even in animation stories; and awarding keeps white spaces white, too. Not much of a surprise, yet annoying nevertheless. But as for Chris Rock, the "real question everybody wants to know in the world is: Is Hollywood racist? You know. You gotta go at that at the right way. Is it burning-cross racist? No. Is it 'Fetch me some lemonade' racist? No! It's a different type of racist." (quote from: Fallon 2017)

And, yes it is, racist, I mean. In Sci-Fi, too. So if it is logical to assume that racist exclusion in science-fiction films is not going to be different to any other film made, then one question: what Black people have to do in these films in the first place?

Well: this is not just about Hollywood, of course. It's global and seemingly omnipotent. Even science-fiction films made and set in South Africa, have not fared any better, the two main stories "District 9" (2009) and "Chappie" (2015) are incredible in their use of blackness, their use and isolation of Black bodies, and the choices made where main characters are concerned and conceived. In "District 9" the "Nigerians" are presented as gun-running criminals and cannibalistic xeno-prostitutes, with whiteness remaining at the center of the narrative; while "Chappie" simply sidelines blackness, a miracle considering the film's South African setting.

3. Why have Black bodies?

The presence of Black people in science-fiction is complicated when the body is supposed to be subsumed by the scientific mind, and the body-without-organs, a la Deleuze and Guattari (2005), is undeniably and painfully white. This body-without-organs can only be treated as a universal imagined body, and the need to actively describe the literary or virtual body when it is other than white might go some way to explain the representation of the future-black body. This is why, when the geneticist in "Gattaca" (1997) suggests that white parents have a black child, race is inserted into a film where the focus is supposed to be a post-race world where the only indications of good and valid personhood is the tale told by their DNA, which should signify desired physical, social and emotional abilities. And yet this is not the case. Blackness is near-eradicated in this glorious near future, with a geneticist telling prospective "parents" that all potentially prejudicial conditions have been removed from their soon coming blue-eyed, dark-haired, and fair-skinned son. In a scenario like this blackness is deeply complicated in its plea for relevance and desirability, with the Black actor, Blair Underwood, who played the geneticist, implicated in a race-coded narrative of pending self-extinction.

Science-fiction, as representation of the future-past, the future-present, or the future-future, is constructed as a site of technicist whiteness, and the anxiety that emerges when this vision is put under stress is palpable. The plan to boycott "Star Wars: The Force Awakens" (2015) may be amusing in retrospect, but it was a real concern for some. The Guardian reported as follows: "The release of the new Star Wars trailer has been met with excitement online except by a small faction of Twitter users who called for a boycott of the upcoming sequel, claiming it to be 'anti-white propaganda'. The hashtag #BoycottStarWarsVII was started after trolls were angry over the casting of black actor John Boyega, claiming the film was promoting "white genocide.'" (Lee 2015)

The media coverage of #BoycottStarWarsVII garnered points to the level of apprehension already in place regarding the Black body's presence in a science-fiction film. And while the trolls' opinions have been mocked in some quarters, lingering antipathy towards a transforming future found resonance in their observations and conclusion.

This anxiety about the possibility of a changing world imagined in science-fiction is closely described in the 2006 analysis of White Supremacists response to "The Matrix" trilogy carried out by C. Richard King and David J. Leonard and published as "Racing the Matrix: Variations on White Supremacy in Responses to the Film Trilogy." The essay demonstrates how deeply science-fiction imaginings of the future mattered to White Supremacists. Not what one would expect to be the first choice in viewing by White Supremacists, but one response to "The Matrix: Reloaded" (2003) tells of the depth of feeling and anxiety scenes from the film caused: "Zion was like walking into downtown Richmond. Negroes everywhere, only here, they had all the white women. The 'black power fist' seems to be the salute in Zion. And of course, this movie leaves you knowing two things. Only minorities of every creed are smart enough to break free from the Matrix, and only they are smart enough to lead. Only white people are evil enough to create the matrix and maintain it." (King; Leonard 2006: 363) The use of historical stereotypes of blackness by the forum illustrates how closely the writer's experience of their present informs their imagined future. Obsessions with miscegenation remains, and Black revolution is to be feared, even when presented in a fictional setting.

4. Need for perfection

One way of dealing with race and science-fiction, or more correctly with scrutinising the erasure of blackness from science-fiction, is to assume that there is a desire for utopia – a desire and a utopia that narrates about many worlds yet as white unity only, and this is characterised in the way that aliens are presented. Almost without exception, aliens are presented as being the same. This leaves earthlings with little options other than presenting Earth as being the same. It also removes the need to explain current lived, and likely future incarnations of life on Earth for the viewer. So, while filmmakers may argue they do not mean to expunge blackness from these future-places they create, the people that make it onto the screen reveal an altogether different intention.

Utopias, as places of perfect and yet unvisited existence, are important within this debate, even if science-fiction films maintain an obsession with dystopia, with social, technological, and political failure being better suited to address deep-seated fears held by both the makers and consumers of science-fiction. However, anxieties around race soon seep into these platonic constructions, shaping the forms the utopia in place, or the world-gone-wrong, takes. So, an ostensibly benign three-part tale aimed at teenage readers, "The Hunger Games" (2012-2015) (a clear derivative of "Battle Royal" (2000)), easily positions a resolved hero in a post-apocalyptic United States of America into a political and material reality, where racial segregation is still designated, to District 11 – the plantation district. One can further look at the situation where the inventors of the New Founding Fathers do much to address the question of blackness being symbolic of poverty and its justified elimination, as an imagined new United States seeks to rationalise its anger towards itself and others within another film series, "The Purge" (2013; 2014; 2016). In these films, whiteness is deeply and continuously reinforced as the holder of beauty, privilege and wealth. And even if momentarily a group of black people questions state-sanctioned mass-murder, they are only set up to serve the coming real hero in the form of whiteness wronged in its innocence. In line with the discursive and structural power of white supremacy, the systematic elimination of blackness is treated as "normal" by directors and critics alike. For example, in the third part of the trilogy "The Purge: Election Year" (2016), the death of the two main Black characters can be seen as a normalising device of Africanism to pave the way for another day not disturbed by racial difference and aspiration that does not know its proper place. It is worth remembering that in the first instalment of the series it is the intrusion of a Black character into a white home that upsets the idyllic, if violent fantasy, of a new world were whiteness is rendered safe and secure by unrestrained slaughter.

5. Enjoy the view

Whether the reader/viewer of science-fiction narratives wants to or not, they are forced into having and maintaining a hegemonic and unified worldview. This is crucial in ensuring the presented new or alternative world being constructed is perceived as either desirable or disagreeable. It is imperative to give viewers ideology they can align themselves to. At the least, and for good reason, one of the most popular forms of science-fiction, is humanity in defence of the survival of humanity. At that level of need all internal divisions are supposed to disappear. It is easy to assume inevitable human solidarity in the face of an alien invasion, but this is a myth perpetuated within science-fiction. If one takes a close look at this alleged solidarity in "Independence Day" (1996), the highest grossing film of 1996, the Africans merely jump up and down in the Savannah at the moment of crisis. And things do not get much better in "Independence Day: Resurgence" made 2016. Set twenty years after the first alien invasion, Africans are characterised as brave, if stubborn warriors led by a "warlord" capable of taking on technologically advanced aliens with two cutlasses, from behind. This inability to engage with technology is made all the more obvious when the character played by Geoff Blum says to the alien-weapon-toting Africans "I see you've found their armoury." (Independence Day: Resurgence: 10:23) This is of significance when the fictional president of the United States had previously made the claim that they (and here "they" clearly stands for all people on the planet) have cracked and put the alien technology to good "global" use. In spite of an alien vessel remaining on their "land" "the Africans" (whoever that is) are shown to be still at a first level of utilisation of alien technology, and there is no evidence of "development" in "their homeland". This also means the filmmakers Dean Devlin, Harald Kloser, and Roland Emmerich do not have to deal with the clearly confusing oxymoron of the possible "Black scientist", following on Ron

Posnock's essay, "How It Feels to Be a Problem: Du Bois, Fanon, and the 'Impossible Life' of the Black Intellectual" (1997). And this is within films that Will Smith and his filmic son have leading roles, but their fictional personae appear to be normalised by nationality, when in contestation with other possible black bodies.

6. There is always love

One of the earliest films that depicts a post-apocalyptic Black character, is the 1959 film "The World, the Flesh and the Devil". Here one is confronted with a rather difficult set of understandings of what the end of the world will mean while not dwelling on who represents each part of the film's title. The film's name, which is linked to the three enemies of the soul as defined by Christian tradition, force the viewer to consider the place of the eventual three players. Within the film, the character played by Harry Belafonte, Ralph Burton, can only be representative of the world and labour. He is the one who is handy, and who sets about trying to save what he finds in the world. This leaves the character Sarah Crandall, the self-declaring white woman with unlimited choice, standing in for flesh and temptation, with Benson Thacker, the white male to be waited on hand and foot, as the devil who brings confusion and murderous intent into the new Eden that radioactive isotopes created.

Sarah Crandall expresses her fears that she will never marry to the then last eligible man on earth because he is Black, and in that moment, the possibility of a continuation of humankind ends, until possibility is rekindled at the arrival of Thacker, which heralds the potential continuation of whiteness and the disappearance of blackness. This is undoubtedly comforting to some viewers who see order restored with the potential white family being served by a Black man. This is until Public Enemy reminds us all on their title track on "Fear of a Black Planet" (1990) that fearing a Black planet is ultimately all about love:

"Man you need to calm down, don't get mad
I don't need your sista
But suppose' she said she loved me
Would you still love her or would you dismiss her
What is pure? Who is pure?
Is it European? I ain't sure
If the whole world was to come through peace and love
Then what would we be made of?" (01:12-01:30)

7. Black face in hyperspace

If there is dismissal of blackness in science-fiction, then one has to assume that blackness is allowed onto the screen to perform a role. This role is to play the part of a Black person, a body that carries significance to offset the ideal future whiteness imagines for itself.

Hyperspace only exists in the imagination, this fourth dimension where space can fold, or be folded to take earthlings on temporal and spatial adventures. The great thing about hyperspace is that anything can happen within spaces that do not exist, and what does happen is easy to accept as it is not complicated by having to face "reality" – and yet it may, in the long run, because the hyper-space is as real as the imaginary: it keeps commenting and affecting and reproducing or changing who we are; and who we will be.

So, within hyperspace Ray Bradbury can send all the Black people in the American South to Mars in rockets in "Way in the Middle of the Air"(1950) (and by his own extension, all Black people in the United States, in "The Other Foot"(1951)), and Richard Pryor can send all white people to the moon in "Live & Smokin'" (1985). This narration about the future can be ignored, but it is out there, saying: "I'm glad I'm black. I'd hate to be white. 'Cause y'all got to go to the moon. Ain't no n*ggers going to the moon, you know that. First of all, there ain't no n*ggers qualified. Or so you all tell us. So we don't have to worry about that. If n*ggers was hip, they'd help y'all get to the moon. 'Hey, let's organize and help them white motherfuckers get to the moon. So they leave us alone!'" (Live & Smokin' 1985: 08:07)[15]

Works Cited
Abrams, Jeffrey Jacob (Director). *Star Wars: The Force Awakens*. USA 2015.
Blomkamp, Neill (Director). *Chappie*. Mexico; USA 2015.
Blomkamp, Neill (Director). *District 9*. Canada; New Zealand; South Africa; USA 2009.
Blum, Michael (Director). *Live & Smokin'*. USA 1985.
Bradbury, Ray. "Way in the Middle of the Air." *The Martian Chronicles*. Bradbury, Ray. New York: Doubleday 1950.
Bradbury, Ray. "The Other Foot." *The Illustrated Man*. Bradbury, Ray. New York: Doubleday 1951.
Cameron, James (Director). *Terminator*. USA 1984.
Cameron, James (Director). *Terminator 2 Judgment Day*. USA 1991.
Cameron, James (Director). *Terminator: Salvation*. USA 2009.

---

15 editors note: Because we can't know for sure if the n-word here is used in an empowered reclaiming way, we've decided to edit it // edition assemblage

David, Saul (Director). *Logan's Run*. USA 1976.
Deleuze, Gilles; Guattari, Félix. *A Thousand Plateaus: Capitalism and Schizophrenia*. Minneapolis: University of Minnesota Press 2005.
DeMonaco, James (Director). *The Purge*. USA 2013.
DeMonaco, James (Director). *The Purge: Anarchy*. USA 2015.
DeMonaco, James (Director). *The Purge: Election Year*. USA 2016.
Emmerich, Roland (Director). *Independence Day*. USA 1996.
Emmerich, Roland (Director). *Independence Day: Resurgence*. USA 2016.
Fallon, Patrick. "Chris Rock's Opening Oscar Monologue: A Transcript." *The New York Times* 20.02.2017. https://www.nytimes.com/2016/02/29/movies/chris-rock-monologue.html?_r=0, accessed 17 March 2017.
Fukasaku, Kinji (Director). *Battle Royale*. Japan 2000.
hooks, bell. *Black Looks: Race and Representation*. New York: Routledge 2015.
Jordan, A. Van. "The Brother from Another Planet." *Callaloo* 35.1 (2012): 4-6.
King, C. Richard; Leonard, David J. "Racing the Matrix: Variations on White Supremacy in Responses to the Film Trilogy." *Cultural Studies: Critical Methodologies* 6.3 (2006): 354-369.
Lawrence, Francis (Director). *The Hunger Games: Catching Fire*. USA: 2013.
Lawrence, Francis (Director). *The Hunger Games: Mockingjay – Part 1*. USA: 2014.
Lawrence, Francis (Director). *The Hunger Games: Mockingjay – Part 2*. USA: 2015.
Lee, Benjamin. "Twitter trolls urge boycott of Star Wars over black character." *The Guardian* 20.10.2015. https://www.theguardian.com/film/2015/oct/20/twitter-trolls-boycott-star-wars-black-character-force-awakens-john-boyega#:~:text=The%20release%20of%20the%20new,%E2%80%9Canti%2Dwhite%20propaganda%E2%80%9D, accessed 20 March 2017.
MacDougall, Ranald (Director). *The World, the Flesh and the Devil*. USA 1959.
Morrison, Toni. *Playing in the Dark: Whiteness and the Literary Imagination*. New York: Vintage 2015.
Mostow, Jonathan (Director). *Terminator 3: Rise of the Machines*. USA 2003.
Niccol, Andrew (Director). *Gattaca*. USA 1997.
Outkast. *ATLiens*. USA: LaFace Records; Sony BMG 1996.
Posnock, Ross. "How It Feels to Be a Problem: Du Bois, Fanon, and the 'Impossible Life' of the Black Intellectual." *Critical Inquiry* 23.2 (1997): 323-349.
Pryor, Richard. *Bicentennial Nigger*. USA: Warner Bros. 1976.
Public Enemy. *Fear of a Black Planet*. USA: Def Jam; Columbia 1990.
Ross, Gary (Director). *The Hunger Games*. USA 2012.
Sayles, John (Director). *The Brother from Another Planet*. USA 1984.
Sun Ra. *We Travel the Space Ways*. USA: El Saturn Records ca. 1967.
Taylor, Alan (Director). *Terminator Genisys*. USA 2015.
Wachowski, Lana; Wachowski, Lilly (Directors). *The Matrix*. Australia; USA 1999.

Wachowski, Lana; Wachowski, Lilly (Directors). *The Matrix Reloaded*. USA 2003.
Wachowski, Lana; Wachowski, Lilly (Directors). *The Matrix Revolutions*. USA 2003.